Fostering Student Accountability Through Student-Led Conferences

by Patti Kinney

Foreword by Rick Stiggins

AMLE.

Association for Middle Level Education
Westerville, Ohio
www.amle.org

National Association of Secondary School Principals
Reston, Virgina
www.nassp.org

Library of Congress Cataloging-in-Publication Data

Kinney, Patti, 1952-
   Fostering student accountability through student led conferences / Patti Kinney.
      p. cm.
   Includes bibliographical references.
   ISBN 978-1-56090-249-2
   1. Student-led parent conferences. 2. Portfolios in education. I. Title.
   LC225.5.K55 2012
   371.19'2--dc23
                              2012026178

Contents

*Additional forms and handouts are available at www.amle.org/SLC_Kinney.

Acknowledgements

A book is not written in isolation—it is the assemblage of the thoughts, practices, and wisdom of others, and I am deeply grateful to those colleagues and friends who have helped in this work.

This book would not exist if Pam Sessions, Marybeth Munroe, and I had not co-authored *A School-wide Approach to Student-led Conferences* (NMSA 2000). Their work in creating and articulating the process developed in the 1990s at Talent Middle School served as the strong foundation for the rewriting and updating of this book.

This book also would not have been possible without the ongoing effort of the staff, students, and parents at Talent Middle School in the Phoenix-Talent School District in southern Oregon. They were truly on the cutting edge of this process.

I am extremely grateful for the contributions and help from:

The authors of the case studies that illustrate not only the growth of student-led conferences over the years but also their ability to work at all grade levels.

- Amanda Blaine and Morgan Cuthbert, 7th grade teachers, Harrison Middle School, Yarmouth, ME

- Jay Clark, principal, Van Buren Middle School, Van Buren, OH

- Theresa Hinkle, teacher (retired), John R. Kernodle Middle School, Greensboro, NC

- Kristin Nori, elementary teacher, Charlotte, NC

- Pam Sessions, media specialist, Phoenix High School, Phoenix, OR

- Linda Scott, principal, Oscar Smith Middle School, Chesapeake, VA

John Nori and Pete Reed, two of my colleagues at NASSP, for serving as sounding boards and wordsmith experts when I was searching for just the right word.

Technology consultants Chris Toy and Dedra Stafford for sharing their ideas on how student-led conferences can be enhanced through the use of technology.

Richard Stiggins for his willingness to write the foreword to the book. I have long been a fan of his work and was greatly honored when he graciously agreed to help.

And finally, thank you to Carla Weiland at AMLE. This book is undoubtedly stronger and more useable due to her questions, suggestions, and editing abilities.

Foreword

I have watched parents moved to tears with pride and surprise by their children's leading their own conferences. Most stunning was the reaction of a building principal from another district observing his kindergarten son acting like a little adult in describing to Dad and Mom how he had grown— with actual examples of his work to back it up. Afterward, his dad told me he couldn't believe this was possible and that he was seeing a new side of his son. He was sold on the value of student-led conferences, and his plan was to carry the concept back to his own team.

But sealing the deal for me was an even more compelling story that I was told: When his early evening conference time arrived, a Hispanic student arrived with his extended family in tow to share his learning—Mom, Dad, Gramma, two brothers and two sisters, all younger than he. After introducing them all to his teacher, he seated them at the conference table and retrieved his portfolio from the file. Then, to the teacher's surprise, he began conducting the meeting in Spanish; later the teacher found out the use of Spanish was to honor his grandmother, who spoke no English. The family's attention was sharply focused throughout, and questions were frequent—especially from Gramma. At the end, as they filed out of the room, Gramma, with tears in her eyes, came to the teacher and simply took her hand and squeezed it. Obviously, the conference had been a success. I still become emotional when I tell this story.

The stories above reveal the immense power of student-led conferences to influence student learning. Treat students of any age like adults, and they will prepare and behave like adults. In this book Patti does an outstanding job of guiding practitioners through the entire process of getting buy-in, planning, conducting, and following up on student-led conferences. I will say more about her presentation in a minute. But first, some advice from my experience on how to do this well.

Those who are considering implementing student-led conferences absolutely must approach it with a clear vision of what it takes to do it right, because I promise that, if you do it wrong, you won't get a second shot. And it's too powerful an idea to waste with shoddy application. As Patti points out, it takes a sharply focused sense of purpose. You need to be doing it to provide students with a context within which to articulate their own growth and areas in need of improvement, because it puts them in control of their own academic well-being—and if you don't define lifelong learner in those terms, I don't know how you define it.

Productive student-led conferencing also requires crystal clear learning targets that are completely understood by both students and teachers from the beginning of the learning. Students need to know where they are headed, where they are now, and how to close the gap between the two. Their conferences are entirely about their progress in narrowing that gap.

Productive conferencing requires that teachers bring to the process a solid foundation of assessment literacy. They need to be able to use high-quality assessments to generate accurate evidence of student learning that feeds into portfolios and the communication process. We do little good to provide students with evidence that misrepresents the truth about their growth.

And finally, this communication system relies on adherence to principles of effective communication in a formative assessment context. Those principles are not the same as communicating summative assessment results. Formative applications bank on descriptive, not judgmental, feedback. Students must have the conceptual understanding, vocabulary, and knowledge of assessment results needed to tell the story of their own journey to academic success. Again, they need to be prepared to communicate where they are headed, where they are now, and how much the gap has closed due to their efforts.

Teachers need to be masters of the concept of "assessment FOR learning" (AFL) in which we use assessment to support learning, not merely to monitor and grade it. AFL is formative assessment with deep student involvement. In AFL classrooms, students understand (one more time!) where they're headed with their learning, where they are now, and how THEY plan to close the gap between the two. When students become partners in the formative assessment process, their achievement skyrockets. All students gain, with the largest gains accruing for low achievers. Use the assessment literacy professional development programs cited by Patti—it is essential that faculties develop a strong foundation of professional competence in this domain.

The great strength of this book is that Patti lays out the path to successful conferences in realistic and practical terms. She describes the underlying psychology of learning that drives the system, along with the cost/benefit of implementing the student-led conferencing format. The costs, of course, are in the faculty time and energy needed to learn about, prepare for, and conduct conferences. The benefits take the form of profoundly increased student engagement, motivation, and, ultimately, achievement. Patti provides real-world illustrations of how these realities play out, describing the effects on teachers, students, parents, and faculties. Finally, she details the keys to effective leadership of faculties who embrace the idea of student involvement in the conferencing process.

There is no greater reward for teachers than to watch their students effectively describe their learning success and take responsibility for their learning challenges in the presence of those whose opinion of them students care most about. That is what student-led conferencing is all about.

Rick Stiggins
Retired Executive Director, Pearson Assessment Training Institute
Portland, Oregon

- THINK A TASKS FOR PORTFOLIO
- HAVE SECTION FOR (S) to think of next steps
- CLASS TIME TO PREP FOR CONFERENCES

- P/T CONF. LUNCH / DINNER
        (S) bring a dish to share
        + people need in cafeteria

- could we do it @ a 6:30 pm slot on
        another day

Introduction

When *A School-Wide Approach to Student-Led Conferences*, the foundation
for this book, was published in 2000, student-led conferences were rare,
especially at the middle and high school levels. Most schools used a
traditional approach of parents and teachers meeting together to discuss
student progress with nary a student in sight. And while the traditional
approach is still common, more and more schools—of all grade levels—
have made the shift to student-led conferences as an authentic way of
teaching students how to become self-reflective, self-evaluative learners
and communicate that learning to others.

The process of students leading conferences was originally implemented
at Talent Middle School (OR) before the No Child Left Behind era, a time
when regulations for state and national school accountability were hardly
a blip on the horizon. Yet, even then we saw student-led conferences as
much more than a communication system with parents; at its heart it was
designed to hold students accountable for their learning. In 1999, assessment
expert Richard Stiggins validated our belief when he said the student-led
conference process

> …is the biggest breakthrough in communicating about
> student achievement in the last century. When students are
> well prepared over an extended period to tell the story of
> their own success (or lack thereof), they seem to experience
> a fundamental shift in their internal sense of responsibility for

that success. The pride in accomplishment that students feel when they have a positive story to tell and tell it well can be immensely motivational. The sense of personal responsibility that they feel when anticipating what it will be like to face the music of having to tell their story of poor achievement can also drive them to productive work. (p. 196)

This book is not designed to be a recipe for student-led conferences, but rather a sharing of the ingredients that must be considered for them to be successful. Because there is no one-size-fits-all approach to their implementation, schools must look at their staff, their students, and their community and then decide how the conferences can effectively work within their situations. As the practice of student-led conferences has spread, it's been rewarding to hear stories of how schools have taken the ideas contained in the original book and made them their own. We hope you enjoy reading the story of Talent Middle School as well as the stories of others who have taken a similar journey.

 Chapter 1

Setting the Stage

It's parent-teacher conference time, and there's a sense of urgency in the air. Hurried conversations occur across tables. While parents stand around impatiently glancing at their watches and waiting their turns, the sound of chimes breaks into the hum of voices. Conversations are quickly cut off as people shuffle from one place to another. Another round of conferences has begun. Teachers are available, sitting at tables packed together in the commons area. Looking around the crowded room, one sees that some teachers will face a never-ending stream of parents, while others sit idly for long periods of time. And, despite the fact that conversations revolve around the progress of students, there's a curious lack of students present.

Sound familiar? If you attend conferences at most schools, you would observe a similar scene hour after hour, day after day. Instead, imagine the following scenario at your school.

Students and parents enter the school together and are welcomed at the front door. They arrive at the conference room, and after a brief introduction to the conference facilitator, the conference begins by students reading a letter written to their parent or guardian (see Figure 1-1).

Figure 1-1 *Sample student letter to parent or guardian*

Mom and Dad,

Thank you for coming to my student-led conference. I have worked on many projects this trimester and have done my work with better organization. My favorite piece of work is my coffee-stained book cover. I like it because I spent a lot of time and put a lot of hard work into it. My next favorite is band because I'm doing a good job on the French horn.

Again, I'm glad you came to my conference. I hope it lets you see all of the things I do in school (only the good things I hope).

At the end of this conference I have two goals written. It would be nice if you would write a third one with me.

Sincerely,

As the conference continues, the student leads his or her parents through a prepared portfolio of work, sharing and discussing the skills, processes, and content learned by doing each piece. The conference ends with the student and parents setting goals for the rest of the school year. For most of the conference, the facilitator has remained in the background, stepping in only when needed.

Student-led conferences (SLCs) began at Talent Middle School (TMS) in Oregon in the early 90s when two teachers used the process with their language arts-social studies classes. As they shared the results with the staff, interest and excitement grew, and more teachers joined in each year until 1996, when the staff made the decision and planned for all students and teachers to participate in the process. This book tells the story, describes the plan, and provides you with support to make SLCs a reality at your school. But first, let's look at why this change in conferencing procedures is necessary.

Purpose of SLCs

Those who work in middle schools know that early adolescence can be a trying time for young people (and the adults around them) as students struggle with issues of identity and independence. Taking these developmental needs into account is critical to designing effective assessment procedures. *This We Believe: Keys to Educating Young Adolescents* (National Middle School Association [NMSA], 2010), the position paper of Association for Middle Level Education (AMLE), identifies the essential characteristics of middle grades schools and states:

> Means of assessing student progress should also serve a learning function, helping students to clarify their understandings and providing information on which to base judgments. Grades alone are inadequate for reporting student progress...An important part of student self-assessment is reflecting on personal growth and learning, communicating what they have learned, and identifying further learning goals. Student-led conferences are especially valuable in achieving the goals of an assessment and reporting program. (pp. 25–26)

Additionally, at its heart, student-led conferencing is about helping students learn to be more accountable for their learning, an ongoing task that runs the gamut of grade levels K–12. *Breaking Ranks: The Comprehensive Framework for School Improvement* (National Association of Secondary School Principals [NASSP], 2011) provides K–12 schools with a framework designed to improve collaboration and student learning and to personalize the school environment. Many of the framework's recommendations can be addressed through the process of SLCs.

While the purpose of the traditional parent-teacher conference is admirable, it does little to promote the development of confident, self-directed learners and to make long-term impact on academic improvement. Although a primary purpose of parent-teacher conferences has been to encourage students to accept more responsibility for their learning and their actions, ironically, students rarely have been involved in the process. Instead of being invited to participate in discussions regarding their school progress (or lack thereof), students have been left at home to wonder what was being said behind their backs or to worry about which of their misdeeds the teachers would tell their parents. SLCs shift the focus back to where it belongs—on the student.

Research supporting SLCs

Research has shown that the benefits of SLCs far outweigh the effort needed to create these successful experiences for students. Benefits of this process noted by Hackmann (1996, 1997), Stiggins (1994), and Babar and Tolensky (1996) include:

- Students engaged in self-evaluation are more highly motivated to produce quality work.

- Students' skills of organization, leadership, and public speaking are strengthened.

- Students are empowered to make improvement through the goal-setting process.

- Home and school share the responsibility for supporting student achievement.

- The conference itself is a form of authentic assessment that increases the students' accountability and responsibility for learning.

- Students have the opportunity to learn and practice skills of evaluation and reflection.

- Positive communication between parent and student is fostered.

- A significantly higher percentage of parents attend SLCs than parent-teacher conferences.

- Students' self-confidence and self-esteem increase.

- Students and parents have a clearer understanding of the expectations for student learning.

A more recent multiple case study completed in 2009 by Judith Hoeppner, Director of Curriculum and Instruction in Campbellsport School District, Wisconsin, found a close alignment between 21st century learning skills and the benefits of student-led conferencing.

> The results of greater student communication skills, self-confidence, responsibility, self-assessment, metacognition, and accountability reported by teacher, parent, and fourth grade student participants are closely associated with the students' mastering life and career skills, which are key elements of 21st century learning. Effective communication, on a local and global basis, includes joint effort, collaboration, and interpersonal skills with strong underpinnings that is personal, social, and civic responsibility. (personal communication June 11, 2012)

Collectively, these are impressive benefits and support practices recognized as appropriate for the middle school years (NMSA, 2010), and they match the recommendations for overall school improvement detailed in *Breaking Ranks: The Comprehensive Framework for School Improvement* (2011). As we continue to unravel the process of student-led conferences, we hope you come to agree with the words of one parent:

> These conferences are great! I'm impressed by (my child's) ability to reflect on his learning, his strengths, and his weaknesses. Keep it up! I really like the self- evaluation aspect of the conference. It is a great tool and can be a skill used throughout his school career.

 Chapter 2

Begin with the End in Mind

Ownership. Accepting responsibility. It seems as if this goal is often at the center of much of what we do as educators. In our practices and procedures, we continually strive to seek better ways to teach students to accept responsibility for their part in the learning process. Research and a wealth of experience tell us that using authentic methods of assessment, that is, measuring a student's abilities and/or achievements in relatively real-life contexts, is an important key to teaching students how to learn and engage as a partner in the learning process. Authentic assessments typically involve students actively demonstrating their learning by creating products, portfolios, or performances which are then self- and teacher-assessed. These assessments challenge the student with tasks that are potentially worthwhile, significant, and meaningful to both the student and others. Chappuis, Stiggins, Chappuis, & Arter (2012) informs us that when we teach students to understand and demonstrate key dimensions of performance, we prepare them to achieve the targets we value. This, in turn, leads to higher academic performance and accountability. At TMS, the desire to help students take more responsibility for their learning led to the implementation of school-wide SLCs.

When Talent Junior High became a middle school in 1990, one thing that remained the same was arena-styled parent-teacher conferences. Teachers gathered in a common space, and parents were scheduled for 10-minute conferences with up to three teachers. Math and language arts teachers had long lines waiting to see them, while others sat for long periods of time with no visitors. Attendance for the conferences was about 40% (mostly parents of higher-performing students), conversations were hurried, the atmosphere was chaotic, very few of the non-English speaking parents in our school community were in attendance, and there was a severe lack of privacy—and although the conversations were about students, there was rarely a student in sight. We knew if we sincerely wanted to improve learning on a larger scale and better involve parents in the process, something had to change.

Two teachers approached the administration with an idea. At a conference, they had heard about elementary schools holding SLCs, and they were interested in seeing if they would work at the middle level. These teachers wanted students not only to be a part of the conferences, but also to lead the conversations with parents during the conferences. Their hope was to give students ownership and pride in their learning by presenting their strengths, weaknesses, and aspirations, and to hold a more thoughtful and productive dialogue than the traditional parent-teacher conference permits.

Starting the process

Given the go-ahead, the teachers researched the possibilities, devised a process, taught their students the necessary skills, and implemented the conferences. It was a resounding success and garnered the interest of others on staff. The school continued to examine other ways to improve the conferencing process, but within a few years, enough teachers were embracing the student-led process that the leadership team felt it was time to make a school-wide shift to this way of conferencing.

Careful planning and collaboration as a staff helped ensure that the first attempt to use this as a school-wide practice was a successful one. Together, the staff examined the best way to organize the conferences to ensure a smooth implementation. Equity of assignments was a major concern, and many discussions were held to find a way to ensure that everyone would have a fair share of the workload. Out of these discussions came a structure that had every certified staff member (administrators included) serving as a conference facilitator for an equal number of students. We devised a schedule to provide a "drop-in" time period between SLCs to address concerns of parents interested in visiting specific teachers. A timeline for implementation made expectations clear. Even as staff worked together to design the implementation plan, as is always the case with making changes, some members were reluctant to try the new process. The group acknowledged their concerns and promised an evaluation of the process. But the message was clear: the school was moving in this direction, and the expectation was for everyone to contribute to its success. Immediately after the first school-wide implementation, staff, parents, and students evaluated the process, and the staff used the results to adjust the process the following year. Interestingly, some of the initially reluctant teachers later became the strongest supporters of the process. Today, two principals and nearly twenty years later, the concept is a long-established practice at TMS and serves as a model for others who wish to implement the process.

Keys to success

Collaboration is critical. Just as the conferences help students take ownership of their learning, the staff must have ownership in the process as well. To be successful, they must be ready and willing to take a serious look at changing the format of the traditional conference approach to one that is centered on student participation. Gathering data and perceptions of the current procedures is a good starting point; follow that up by helping stakeholders understand what SLCs are and why they are an educationally sound practice. The professional development kit *The What, Why, & How of Student-Led Conferences* (Berckemeyer & Kinney, 2005) is a good resource for beginning those conversations in your school.

The keys that sustained this practice and made it an integral part of the school culture at TMS included both the up-front planning and work to ensure a successful first time implementation and the continual evaluation and refinements that have occurred over the years. NASSP's *Breaking Ranks:*

A Field Guide for Leading Change (2009) cited this work as an example of how to implement sustainable change by using the figure below to show how our actions illustrated an effective process to guide change.

Figure 2-1 *Model of process to implement student-led conferences*

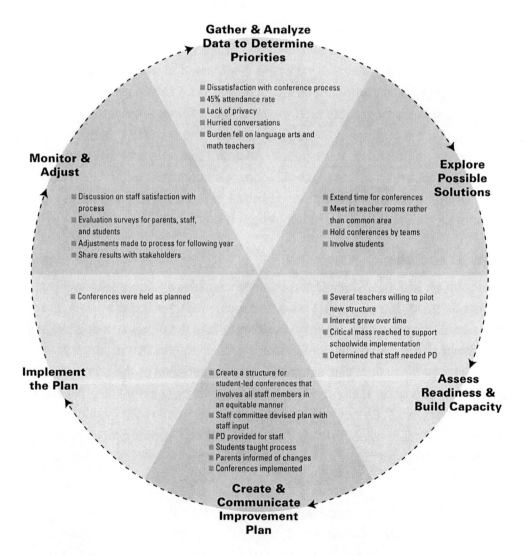

Gather & Analyze Data to Determine Priorities
- Dissatisfaction with conference process
- 45% attendance rate
- Lack of privacy
- Hurried conversations
- Burden fell on language arts and math teachers

Explore Possible Solutions
- Extend time for conferences
- Meet in teacher rooms rather than common area
- Hold conferences by teams
- Involve students

Monitor & Adjust
- Discussion on staff satisfaction with process
- Evaluation surveys for parents, staff, and students
- Adjustments made to process for following year
- Share results with stakeholders

- Conferences were held as planned

Assess Readiness & Build Capacity
- Several teachers willing to pilot new structure
- Interest grew over time
- Critical mass reached to support schoolwide implementation
- Determined that staff needed PD

Implement the Plan
- Create a structure for student-led conferences that involves all staff members in an equitable manner
- Staff committee devised plan with staff input
- PD provided for staff
- Students taught process
- Parents informed of changes
- Conferences implemented

Create & Communicate Improvement Plan

National Association of Secondary School Principals. (2009). *Breaking Ranks: A Field Guide for Leading Change.*

Unfortunately, implementing school improvement initiatives can be messy and doesn't necessarily follow a linear plan…or a circle, for that matter. When putting initiatives such as SLCs into practice, you may suddenly discover that you've left out a piece and have to backtrack…and as soon as you begin to monitor and adjust, you need to start gathering and analyzing data again. Thus, rather than a line, which has a beginning and an end, we diagram this change process as circular to graphically represent continuous activity. Since every school has its own DNA, the school's culture, combined with situational demands, requires you to make adjustments to the change process.

Schools choosing to implement school-wide student-led conferences will need to make many critical, up-front decisions. A smooth, well-organized introduction will go a long way toward convincing your staff, students, and parents of its many benefits. In creating a structure for your school, you must keep in mind the needs of your staff, your students, and your parents. Although every school's plan will differ, do consider the elements discussed below.

Why and when?

Before you decide when and how often to hold student-led conferences, determine why you are making the changes and what you wish to accomplish. Clarifying your outcomes will help define the conference process for your school.

Although schools can hold conferences at any time of year, most prefer either fall and/or spring. Fall conferences tend to be future-directed, while spring conferences are more summary-oriented. Some schools choose to do SLCs once a year; others, twice. Regardless of the timing and frequency, students should know when their work is going to be gathered for a conference and the conference preparation timeline. This builds ownership in the process and helps students realize they are major players in the success of this process. As you think through the implementation of SLCs at your school, determining "why" and "when" will help you develop the best format and organization for your conferences.

Who will facilitate?

While students will play the central role in the actual conference, an adult will serve as the facilitator. The role of the facilitator is to help students prepare for the conference, especially at the elementary and middle school levels, and to be present during the conferences. This means you must determine who will play the role of the facilitator. At the elementary level, this responsibility generally falls on the student's grade-level teacher. At the middle and high school levels, possibilities include organizing by teams, homerooms, advisory teachers, or choosing a set period (e.g., everyone facilitates his or her fifth period class).

At TMS, every certified staff member serves as a facilitator. Teachers, administrators, counselors, media specialist, etc., are randomly assigned students with approximately equal numbers of sixth, seventh, and eighth graders. The students remain with the same facilitator for their three years in middle school; each fall a staff member's eighth graders are replaced with incoming sixth graders and students new to the school. In making those assignments, we did our best to ensure that each facilitator worked with about the same number of students and also carefully considered the placement of students with special needs to keep the workloads balanced.

Although this system works well, there are issues to consider if you contemplate using a similar plan. First, because the initial assignment was random, the facilitator of our conferences was not always a current content area teacher of the student. In the beginning this was a concern, but as the years passed, it has not been an issue. Second, if everyone serves as a facilitator, someone may not always be available to troubleshoot during conferences if the need arises. While rare, there have been times when it would have been helpful to have an administrator available to assist with a "sticky" situation. A possible solution is to have a district administrator present in the building or stagger the conference schedule of the administrators to ensure someone is always available to help if needed.

As you determine how your school will handle assigning facilitators, look at your school's structure and see what is already in place that can be adapted. Consider the issue of equity in making your decision: if the staff feels that everyone shares a similar load, ownership and support become less of an issue.

Developing a timeline

Creating a timeline helps prevent those unexpected "surprises" that can derail the process. Early in the school year, a small group of staff representing various groups can meet to decide what needs to be done and when and who will be responsible for doing it. Success lies in the details. Nothing is too small to include—even picky things such as when the forms will be reproduced or who will be responsible for making sure families are scheduled together. After the timeline is created, distribute copies to all those involved in the process. See Figure 2-2 on the next page for a sample.

Scheduling time to prepare students

When developing the timeline, determine how often students and their facilitator should meet to prepare for the conference. If conference facilitators do not meet with their students on a daily basis, you may have to develop a special schedule for conference preparation days. To easily determine how much time is needed for preparation, start with the conference dates and work backwards. To determine your school's needs, think about how much time it will take to get acquainted, organize paperwork, teach the process, write goals, and practice for the conference.

Defining responsibilities

Clearly defining the responsibilities of the student, the conference facilitator, and the classroom teacher will help the process go smoothly. Classroom teachers play two roles, and it is important they know what is expected in each of those jobs. For example, as teachers, they assign their students work that will lend itself to use in a conference, help their students select samples

Figure 2-2 *Sample timeline*

Talent Middle School Student-Led Conferences
Timeline for Staff/Student Preparation

Sept. 7–Nov. 8:   Teach, reflect, and gather sample work to use in conferences.

Oct. 4:   Overview of conference plan with new teachers.

Oct. 11:   Present overview of plan and timeline to staff; departments meet to review cover sheets.

Oct. 20:   Facilitator groups: Get acquainted, share system with new students.

Nov. 1:   Student Services schedules sibling conferences; cover sheets/missing work forms distributed to teachers.

Nov. 3:   Facilitator groups: Schedule students, fill out postcards, return to office.

Nov. 8:   Staff meeting to troubleshoot and discuss last-minute details. Work prepared/practiced: Cover sheets, work, reflections, missing sheets.

Nov. 10:   LA teachers help students write Dear Parent letter. Send on collection days.

Nov. 12:   Grades turned in by end of day. Morning inservice, afternoon for grades.

Nov. 15–19:   Facilitators help students organize all work, fill in table of contents, and write goals. Teach and practice the conference procedure.

Nov. 19:   Facilitator: place report cards in folders. Send home reminder invitation. Make final check to ensure all is prepared.

Nov. 22–24:   **STUDENT-LED CONFERENCES!!!**

Nov. 29:   First day of new trimester.

Dec. 1:   Conference facilitator: Celebrate and have a "How did it go?" discussion.

Dec. 2:   Students pick up portfolio from facilitator at beginning of 1st period. "Unload" file throughout day (some work may need to be kept; the rest can go home).

of work from their classroom portfolios, and give their students opportunities to practice sharing those pieces during class. As facilitators, they schedule the conferences, help students organize their conference portfolios, teach students how to put it all together into smooth presentations, and are present for support during the actual conferences.

Student responsibilities should be spelled out as well. They need to know it is their job to complete the required assignments, evaluate and reflect on their skills as learners, collect the work and take it to the correct places, and prepare themselves to lead effective conferences with their parents or guardians.

Determining conference schedule

Creating a schedule that accommodates the needs of parents is complicated. Because we had parents and teachers who still wanted an opportunity to visit together during the conference days, we created a schedule that allowed for a 30-minute conference followed by a 30-minute "drop-in" period. After the conference, parents who wished to visit with a particular teacher could do so. Initially, some teachers felt they would be overwhelmed by the number parents dropping in; experience has shown that, in reality, most of the visits are of a more casual nature and take up very little time.

Because the student is leading the conference, it is possible to have multiple conferences taking place in the same room at the same time. We typically scheduled up to three simultaneous conferences; four, for the busier evening hours. The number of days and/or hours your district sets aside for parent conferences will also determine your schedule. We were fortunate to have had three days, and because we could be flexible with the time, we accommodated parents' work schedules by conferencing two longer days into the evening and one shorter day. Schools with less time can schedule slightly shorter conferences, reduce or eliminate the drop-in time, and/or hold more simultaneous conferences.

Communicating with parents

Get the word out—school newsletters, school and teacher websites, letters mailed home, e-mails, parent nights, and articles in your local newspapers. Be creative and remember that not all parents get their information in the same manner! The more parents understand the process, the more willing they will be to participate (see Figure 2-3).

Figure 2-3 *Sample article from parent newsletter*

Student-Led Conferences November 23, 24, 25

On November 23, 24, or 25 we are scheduling all students at TMS in student-led conferences. We have used this conference format for the past several years because we believe student involvement in the conference makes learning active, provides opportunities for students to self-reflect and evaluate their performance, and encourages students to accept responsibility for their learning.

Prior to the conferences, students will create portfolios representing their work of the first twelve school weeks. The students will conduct the conference detailing skills and processes they have learned and sharing goals they've set to further improve themselves. Students will learn to select representative work, write self-reflective evaluations, and diagnose their own strengths and weaknesses. Included in each portfolio will be a traditional report card.

We will schedule a 30-minute time block for you and your child to conference. A facilitator, in most cases your child's homeroom teacher, will also attend the conference. Because this is an important experience for all our students, we hope for 100% participation.

Conferences will be scheduled from 7:30 a.m. to 6:30 p.m. on the 23rd, from 10:30 a.m. to 8 p.m. on the 24th, and from 8:00 a.m. to 11:30 a.m. on the 25th. If you wish to speak with specific teachers, a drop-in time will be available during the half-hour prior to and the half-hour following your child's conference.

We will schedule conferences the first week in November. You can help us by telling your child what day and time works best for you. We will confirm your appointment on a postcard mailed to your home. Thank you in advance for supporting your child's education in such an important way.

Building capacity with professional development

As mentioned earlier, student-led conferences began at TMS as a grass roots movement by teachers. Although the teachers and parents involved felt it was successful, moving it to a building level did not happen by accident; it took teaching, modeling, training, and refining. Once the decision was made by the school's site council to go school-wide, intensive planning began to determine the professional development needs of the staff.

For our first staff training in the spring prior to fall implementation, we presented an overview including:

- A researched-based rationale for moving to student-led conferences

- Responsibilities of student, classroom teacher, and the facilitator

- The conference format we would use to maintain consistency

- A timeline of responsibilities/events leading up to the conferences

- A sample schedule

The next professional development session began with a video of a student-led conference. Made for training purposes, the video featured a capable student with two teachers playing the role of parents. During this session, we also discussed the type of work samples that would be used during the conference.

look for online model of SLC

Holding content area meetings led to consistency in the work samples collected from each content area. Collaboratively, they designed the content area cover sheets for the students' portfolios; both students and teachers used the cover sheets to rate learning behaviors of students.

Over the next several months and into the fall, mini-training sessions took place on topics such as scheduling, self-reflections, work sample collection, portfolio organization, writing of "Dear Parent" letters, goal setting, and general conference procedures. We found it best to work from a "need to know" philosophy of professional development. Rather than cover everything at once, we discovered it worked better to give a big picture overview and then teach the smaller pieces just prior to implementation. To some degree, this helped prevent the feeling of being overwhelmed. But, as when implementing any new idea, it was a challenge not to overstress the staff. It was not until the first round of conferences were completed that some of our staff members finally agreed that SLCs were much more effective than the arena-style conferences of the past.

The best advice for training your staff is to keep it simple. Emphasize that most of the procedures used in SLCs are simply an extension of effective teaching practices currently used. Remind them of this. Give as much support, modeling, and encouragement as possible and you will reap the rewards in the end!

Student-Led Conferences in Action: Variation on a Theme

Linda Scott, principal,
Oscar Smith Middle School,
Chesapeake, VA

Bringing student-led conferences (SLCs) to Oscar Smith Middle School was an outcome of a desire to add value to our parent-student conferences and the discovery that the Breaking Ranks framework completely supported this concept. Basing our implementation on the first edition of this book, the staff used it for learning the rationale of SLCs and for developing the school's forms for the process. To begin, I met with groups of staff during their prep periods (core, special education, electives, and physical education teachers as well as paraprofessionals) to discuss the concept of SLCs. It was important that all staff, even those not directly involved, have a voice in the conference process; students and parents had a voice via rating forms and follow-up conferences.

Vision

I first shared my vision of implementing this concept with a volunteer team who would provide leadership as we tweaked the book's process to meet the needs of our students and families. Assuring everyone that I would be there to assist and affirm as they moved into unknown territory, I later found that the volunteer group needed very little guidance from me as they began implementation; I served more as a cheerleader for their efforts.

A team volunteered before they left for the summer break with the goal of implementing the process during the upcoming school year. During break they outlined their implementation process with input from other staff that would be involved. My vision was for these volunteers to take ownership and study the concept. Then they would reach out to their peers and seek others to commit to the concept of SLCs.

Implementation

I met with the team during the summer, and they had all components in place: forms were complete, the process was determined, and the parent letter explaining the concept of SLCs was ready for copying. What a principal's joy! This was clearly going to be group that would spread the concept to other teams.

The teachers were excited about their adaptations to the process and forms. These included:

- Electives and PE teachers developed their own criteria on the input forms and gained ownership in the process.

- Our teachers found it worked best for them if they provided available conference times for parents and had the parent call their child's guidance counselor to set up an interview.

- The school sent parents an informational letter about the SLC process on the first day of school; parents received additional letters with progress reports and report cards.

- Finding it a natural fit with their curriculum objectives, English teachers served as advisors to their own students in preparing students for the process, guiding them in writing their essays, and teaching them how to lead the conferences.

- Students wrote letters about themselves instead of solely writing an introduction to the conference. Keeping their thoughts focused and practicing an essay format, students succinctly addressed each subject in the letters.

- Teachers conducted only one SLC in a room at a time. If parents prompted it or asked questions that went unanswered, facilitators held a "regular" conference after the SLC. These were rare and brief. Scheduling only one at a time allowed time for the teachers to develop confidence in the process.

- Other staff members were involved by standing in for a parent who was not able to attend. This ensured the student was still able to share and set their goals with an adult. Students who conferenced with a "stand-in parent" were very excited about sharing with an adult.

- Students were guided through goal setting at the conference meeting, even if a staff member stood in for the parent. The students wrote the two goals they wanted to achieve, and the parent then gave approval.

Results

Using SLCs resulted in a 15% growth in parent attendance, and we anticipate greater increases as our implementation spreads school-wide. The parents' surveys completed on the spot have shown close to 100% satisfaction with the approach and indicated they liked the opportunity to talk to their child in a different environment. Parents frequently reported that the SLC "provides more structure to attaining goals for the child" and helped their child "remain focused on what he wants to acquire in his educational achievements." They also shared that "this type of conference teaches the student more responsibility."

A "buzz" is happening within our staff. Elective teachers report feeling more involved in the student-parent conference than in past conferences. The teachers implementing the process recognize that this is just a beginning of expanding SLCs school-wide; it is rewarding to hear the excitement from teachers when they talk about the topic! We are moving toward the next step of our vision by sharing our personal experiences of SLCs with the rest of the staff.

Also excited about the conferences, students produced their own video featuring both student and parent voices. In the video, which was shared with the staff, students explained the process, taped a real conference, and concluded with their own critique of SLCs.

Staff professional growth

The excitement generated from SLCs impacted our staff in another way. Although teachers who led the way are excellent teachers, previously they had not enjoyed making formal presentations. Their strong belief in the concept and benefits of SLCs led them to share in front of district middle school principals and offer their guidance and resources to other schools. I have been amazed to see their growth as they have become much more confident in presenting.

SLCs also gave us a vehicle for staff to hear students' perspectives as they share how the characteristics of their teachers and classes encourage their learning. Showing great maturity in their reflections, students, to the surprise of many, did not cast blame on teachers for their "failures" but rather focused on their personal responsibility to make changes. Many were surprised to hear students taking responsibility for a lower grade because they didn't complete assignments even when given many opportunities to do so. Observations of students reflecting in ways that many adults have not yet mastered caused teachers to view students in a new light. A few examples of student comments that raised teacher awareness are:

- "Technology is a fun class that I enjoy. Mr. B is a great teacher and is funny and can laugh at his mistakes. I like a teacher who can do that."

- "I love this class because I get to interact with other students and have fun while I learn."

- "The reason I like Chorus is because I can relate to Ms. D"

- "My teacher gives me the direction needed, and takes us step-by-step. I am responsible for my own behavior. I am choosing to be the clown and joke. If I am going to get better grades, then I need to do better. I have set my goals to do just that."

- "This is my favorite because Orchestra is where I can let out all of my stress and anger. It is the best thing that ever happened to me."

Expanding implementation

Additional teams will implement the conferences in the coming year; my goal is to have additional teams volunteer each year until we have the critical mass needed to take it school-wide. Expansion to other teams will include a similar approach—encouraging them to develop a process that works for their team, adhering to the intent of SLCs, and informing me of their plans. These new teams will also have the added benefit of an experienced group of teachers on staff to provide consultation.

As the instructional leader of our school, I could have taken a swifter approach to implementation and simply declared that SLCs would be implemented school-wide. But by doing that, I would have missed seeing the staff develop their leadership skills, the students give unexpected guidance to teachers in their self-reflections, and the teachers take ownership of the process. The slower, grass-roots approach will help to embed this concept in our school-community culture for a longer-lasting implementation.

 Chapter 3

Meanwhile... Back in the Classroom

As you consider the change to student-led conferences, keep the goal of improving student learning at the forefront in all your decision making. In our case, once the initial organization for SLCs was in place, we then focused on using it to enhance our school's level of instruction in terms of curriculum, instruction, and assessment practices. Experience taught us that a student's demonstrating multiple skills and processes was more effective than showing a piece of work demonstrating a single skill; for example, a research project was more effective than a spelling test.

We found three things that classroom teachers can do to help students prepare for the SLCs are:

- Plan ahead to teach content standards in ways that demonstrate multiple skills and processes.

- Implement the curriculum in a timely manner, so work is completed and prepared for students to use during the conference.

- Teach students how to evaluate and reflect on their work to help them discover and demonstrate who they are as learners.

Plan early

Making thoughtful decisions about curriculum, instruction, and assessment early in the year will make the actual conferences much easier. Because students will discuss their learning in terms of skills and processes, work planned for the conference should:

- Show multiple skills and processes.

- Address adopted content standards.

- Emphasize process as well as quality of product.

- Be examples of "real work" not work contrived for show.

Design work samples

When designing work samples, consider the following questions:

- What outcome(s) will the work sample illustrate?

- Can the work sample, or critical portions of it, be completed in time for the conferences?

- Will the work sample be formative or summative in nature?

- Will teams work together, or will each teacher act individually?

- Will the content be integrated or taught as single subjects?

- What format of a self-reflection will work best for this work sample?

As students complete each project or piece of work, they should complete a self-reflection (see Chapter 4 for more information) to help them clarify what they have learned. By finding discrepancies between what they taught and what the class learned, teachers can use these self-reflections as informal formative assessments providing information to re-teach, review, or reinforce key ideas.

For those wanting to learn more about designing effective work samples, *Authentic Assessment: Active, Engaging Product and Performance Measures* by Sandra Schurr (AMLE, 2012) is an excellent source of information and strategies. In the words of the author, the book was designed to

"...help (educators) align assessment measures (portfolio, product, performance options) with standards-based curriculum by providing active learning strategies that can be used formatively or summatively." (vii)

Organize portfolios

Possible systems for housing work samples and related items include online storage, flash drives, filing cabinets, plastic "milk" crates, banker's boxes, etc. The one that works for you will be based on your style, teaching environment, available space, technology capacity, and budget.

Early in the school year, let parents know that most student work will not come home, but they may set up an appointment to see the portfolio contents at any time. Some teachers make it a practice to ask students to show their work whenever their parents happen to drop by the classroom during the year.

A few weeks prior to conferences

Two to three weeks before conferences, students should select work for the conference portfolio. While it can be either teacher- or student-selected, a mix of teacher-suggested pieces and student selections seems to work best. For example, teachers may want to have all students include a particular unit of study because it illustrates a long-term learning process, but they could let students choose which unit writing piece to include as the best example of their work. Discuss with students the kind of work that makes suitable entries, so they are better able to make good choices. Encourage each student to think through what they have learned and how best to illustrate that for parents. Figure 3-1 outlines suggested work sample criteria.

Figure 3-1 *Sample criteria for work samples*

Student-Led Conference Work Samples

Better Choices: (focus on skills/process)

Writing pieces–including all drafts

Science experiments–including hypotheses, lab notes, and findings

Mathematics problem solving–including process, solution, and proof

Applied mathematics–designing house plans

Book reviews–including summary as well as review of author's style

Research projects–including notes and student-created products

Physical fitness summary–including pre- and post skills, and growth over time

Less Effective Work Samples: (focus on single skills)

Spelling tests*

Answers to chapter questions*

Mathematics timed test*

Multiple choice tests*

These can be included as student choice, but recognize the limitations.

Once the work samples have been chosen for the conference portfolio, students should review previously completed self-reflections to remind them of the thoughts they had while creating the work. Then, they can write summary reflections to articulate growth over time and significant skills learned. It is important to teach students how to share their work and give them ample opportunity to rehearse. Demonstrate how to refer to the work sample for evidence of the skills and processes learned by giving them a highlighter pen to mark a specific passage to share or putting stars or a post-it note next to particular comments on self-reflections to be shared during the conference.

Classroom work samples alone do not always show all that needs to be addressed during a conference. When TMS moved to school-wide conferences, content area teachers across the grade levels designed a cover sheet that listed specific skills and/or behaviors that led to success in their particular subject, e.g., "works safely with lab materials" (science), "reads regularly at home" (language arts), or "dresses down daily" (physical education). Students rated themselves with a +, √, or − on each behavior (see Figure 3-2). Teachers then rated the students and held a conversation with the student if there was a discrepancy. Interestingly enough, students were often much harder at rating themselves than teachers would ever be! Most teacher-student discussions were to acknowledge how well students were doing and to encourage them to rate themselves higher than they originally indicated.

The cover sheets also had a place for teacher remarks, which generally consisted of what we would have told parents if we had met with them. Student behavior and work determined whether the comments were positive or expressed a concern. When teachers needed to discuss serious issues, they wrote notes asking the parents to visit during the drop-in times.

Next, the work samples collected in each subject were stapled behind the cover sheet. The packet was then ready to be collected during the all-school collection time and taken to the facilitator's classroom for the final conference preparation.

Figure 3-2 *Sample specific area cover sheet for conference portfolio*

Core

(Reading, Writing, Speaking, and Social Studies) Cover Sheet

Name: _Maria_   Date: _10-5-12_

Teacher: _Ms. Etienne_   Grade: _7th_

Class Expectations:

+ exceeds expectations   √ meets expectations   − needs improvement

Self Teacher

Self	Teacher	
−	−	Completes classwork/homework on time
√	√	Works independently
+	+	Works well in a group
√	√	Manages behavior appropriately
√	√	Comes to class prepared to learn

Comments: _Maria is doing excellent work in her group in class, but she is having a difficult time completing assignments individually. Please come see me during drop-in time so we can discuss this in more detail._

 Chapter 4

Self-Assessment: Evaluation and Reflection

Art Costa (1989) said,

> We must constantly remind ourselves that the ultimate
> purpose of evaluation is to enable students to evaluate
> themselves. Educators may have been practicing this skill
> to the exclusion of the learners. We need to shift part of this
> responsibility to the students. Fostering students' ability to
> direct and redirect themselves must be a major goal—or what
> is education for? (p. 1)

If we want to develop students that are college-, career-, and citizenship-ready,
then we must give them the skills to both evaluate their performance and
reflect on the learning experience. First, let's look at the differences between
self-evaluation and self-reflection.

Self-Evaluation

Research tells us that self-evaluation is an important skill to teach and
necessary if students are to effectively present themselves as learners
(Paulson & Paulson, 1994). Self-evaluation occurs when students judge the
quality of their performances against standards or other explicit criteria. Their
assessments should be supported by evidence and used to help the students
become more aware of their progress. To do this, teachers, or teachers in
conjunction with students, develop rubrics or scoring guides that clearly state
the criteria. Regardless of how they are developed, it is essential to share the

scoring guides with students prior to their engagement in the work, so they can use it to guide their efforts.

The next step in self-evaluation is for students to learn how to apply the criteria to their own work. Teachers should model this process by providing clear examples of what the pre-determined scoring criteria look like in practice, provide students with multiple opportunities to practice self-evaluation and give feedback on their efforts. Peer assessment can also be a valuable learning experience. For example, a student may rate his or her own piece of writing against criteria previously set and may then trade papers with a classmate and together discuss their perceptions of each others' work.

Self-Reflection

Asking students to reflect on their work should also be an integral part of the learning process. Through self-reflections, students learn to develop insights into their learning and develop the ability to go beyond simply reporting the grade received on an assignment.

The primary purpose of self-reflection is to provide students with a "big picture" view of the learning process and help them articulate not only what they learned, but also how they learned it, and what they can do next to extend and refine their learning. It involves using the knowledge gained through self-evaluation as well as self-knowledge about the performance, such as: What skills, strategies, or techniques did I use? Why did I choose to this particular method? What am I trying to achieve? Am I being successful? How can I change my performance in a desirable way? How can I take what I learned and use it in the future? The purpose of self-reflection is never negative, but encourages honest recognition of strengths, areas to work on, and subsequent goal setting (Smith & Ylvisaker, 1993).

While self-evaluation provides students with a more objective analysis of their performance, self-reflection asks students to take responsibility for their learning, analyze their successes, and identify those areas they want to improve. Teaching students to become more careful and observant partners in their own learning takes them closer to becoming self-managed adults. Students in classrooms where this process is a natural part of the curriculum learn to appreciate what they have accomplished and are better able to set realistic and achievable goals for the future.

A powerful combination

Together, the processes of self-evaluation and self-reflection provide a powerful tool to help students articulate their learning during the SLC. Through self-evaluating and reflecting, students gain a greater appreciation of themselves and a stronger commitment to learning. As students grow and develop the skills of metacognition, they assume greater responsibility and gain intimate information about their learning. Asking them to evaluate and then reflect on a piece of writing, a project, or their learning over a period of time validates their self-knowledge and promotes a sense of collegiality between teacher and student.

Work samples included in the student-led conference portfolio should have evidence of both self-evaluation and self-reflection. The most effective self-evaluation rubrics are developed based on specific content standards and/ or criteria. Those of you wishing to learn more about various strategies and formats for self-evaluations and for information about translating standards into meaningful targets may want to refer to *Effective Classroom Assessment: Linking Assessment with Instruction* by Catherine Garrison, Dennis Chandler, and Michael Ehringhaus (Measured Progress and NMSA, 2009). The remainder of this chapter will focus on the effective use of self-reflections.

Forms of self-reflection

There are many effective and practical ways for students to analyze, evaluate, or comment on their work, thus self-reflections will look very different depending on the ability of the student and the particular assignment. To make self-reflections more meaningful and less of a "canned" exercise, vary their lengths and formats. They may be written or oral and saved electronically or as hard copies. Students need to examine self-evaluations, reflect on individual work, compare similar pieces of work, look at collected work over a significant period of time (a quarter, a semester, or a year), and discuss growth and change. Students may also reflect on their learning in a specific subject area (math, science, social studies, reading) by looking at the skills and processes that are specific to that particular subject area.

For students to become proficient in self-reflection, teachers must teach, model, and reinforce the process. Quality reflections take time, and the value and depth of comments increase when students have ample time to respond thoughtfully. An important word of caution: do not overuse formal, written self-reflections, or students may react negatively and view self-reflection as busywork; use the process wisely and purposefully.

End of product/project self-reflection

When preparing for SLCs, students complete two types of self-reflections. Students write one type at the end of a large project or a significant piece of work. These reflections use data gained from self-evaluations; they focus on the specific content or skills learned through the assignment, the processes or skills used to complete it (i.e., time management, organization, collaboration, etc.), and what the students learned about themselves as learners that can be carried forward into future learning.

Summary self-reflections

Students write a summary self-reflection at the end of a term or semester to show their growth over time. Students easily can do this by reviewing self-reflections from previously completed assignments and explaining how their new work illustrates their growth as a learner.

Teachers can experiment with different forms of reflections to find ones that work best for their subject area and lessons. The types include:

- Writing responses to focused and highly specific questions

- Drawing a picture or webbing the learning process used; showing what was learned and what needs to be done differently next time

- Making a graph of the effort, satisfaction, interest, and value achieved from the project or assignment

- Writing letters to self or teacher

- Writing evaluative essays

- Constructing checklists or charts

- Completing commercially designed reflection forms

- Completing teacher- or student-designed reflection forms

- Engaging in class discussions and one-on-one conferencing

- Using journal entries and responding in learning logs

- Brainstorming

As students learn to self-reflect, they will often become more revealing and better at recognizing and identifying patterns in their own behaviors (e.g., "I tend to procrastinate"), at taking ownership of their learning, and at using specific examples to support their thoughts. They will also begin to make their reflections more multi-dimensional by recognizing strengths and weaknesses, processes and strategies, and skills and knowledge.

Following are two examples of student reflections that illustrate self-reflections used for writing: Figue 4-1 shows an individual reflection on a single piece of work, and Figure 4-2 illustrates a summary reflection of growth over time. You can see how they can be used to show analysis of skills and processes, how skills and processes have changed over time, and how to address the affective areas of learning such as attitudes and beliefs. There are more samples in the Forms and Handouts section at the end of the book.

Figure 4-1 *Sample of single project self-reflection*

Self-Reflection on a Lanuage Arts Project

Name: Date:
Class: Language Arts   Type of Project: ABC Booklet
Title of Project: *The Alice in Wonderland*
ABC Booklet

Whew!!! Your hard work and effort has paid off. You have completed this project to show your understanding of the elements of literature, literary devices, and the content of the novel Alice in Wonderland. *Quite an undertaking, but you are done. Now, please respond thoughtfully to the following questions.*

1. Describe the process you went through to complete the booklet. (Think back to mini-lessons on games/riddles, devices, reading aloud, discussions, finding quotes for your pages, page design, writing and illustrating the booklet, editing, and the people who helped you.)

2. What were your strengths for this project? Examples: creative ideas, comprehension of the novel, personal examples, self-directed learning, time management, understanding of the elements, devices, layout and design, citations.

3. What problems did you encounter and how did you solve them?

4. Rate your understanding of the elements of literature and literary devices on a scale of 1–10.

1   2   3   4   5   6   7   8   9   10
Not at all!   I get it!!

5. When you look at your ABC book, what are you most proud of?

6. What else should I know about your work on this project?

Figure 4-2 *Sample self-reflection of growth over time*

Summary Self-Reflection of Writing

First, look over the writing you have done this trimester, and then thoughtfully answer the questions below. Think of yourself as a writer!

1. What does someone have to do to be a good writer?

   To be a good writer you have to practice, have a good imaginative mind.

2. What is the most important or useful thing you've learned as a writer?

   The most important thing that helps me is to sit in a room with no noise and close my eyes and think.

3. What one thing in writing do you feel more confident about than you did at the beginning of the school year?

   I feel more confident about everything. I never have liked writing, but I think it's fun now.

4. What could you teach someone about writing?

   To not stop, keep going. Something will come up that you like.

5. Which writing trait is your strongest? Why?

   Ideas and content. I have great ideas that are unusual.

6. Which writing trait do you feel is your weakest?

   Voice. I am not good at doing anything with voice. I would like to work on it.

7. Which mode of writing do you enjoy the most? Why?

   Narrative. I am not good at Imaginative. It is much easier for me to write about something that actually happened.

8. What can I as your teacher do to help you be a better writer?

   Do more writing assignments.

9. What kind of writing would you like to do in the future?

   Narrative and persuasive

10. What are your writing goals for the next trimester?

    I have a goal to improve voice on my writing assignments by using better words.

 Chapter 5

Putting the Pieces Together

Think of a SLC as a giant jigsaw puzzle. The teacher's job is to design the shape of the pieces, the student's task is to create them, and now it's the conference facilitator's turn to help students put the parts together to complete the big picture. For this to happen, the facilitator must schedule conferences, collect and organize students' work, ensure "Dear Parent" letters get written and goals get set, and above all—students need to practice, practice, practice!

Much of the organizational, logistics work done to implement SLCs at TMS happened through our student services office. The office manager made certain that the conference facilitators had the necessary materials and information needed to ensure a smooth implementation. In other schools, this has been done by the counseling or administration offices.

Inform parents. Prior to scheduling conferences, inform parents of the conference days and times. Mail a letter home, publish the information in the parent newsletter and on the school's website, send home a flyer with the dates and times, announce it in the daily announcements, or any combination of the above.

Scheduling sheet. Create a scheduling sheet for each facilitator that shows times available for conferences and for drop-ins (if used) (see Figure 5-1). If preventing parents from having to make multiple trips to the school is a priority, schedule siblings first. An easy scheduling method is to compile a list of families and call the oldest child of the family to the office, where the student services' secretary schedules the conferences. After completing this process, the secretary gives the schedule sheets to the conference facilitator along with postcards (color-coded for multiple languages if necessary) and mailing labels (see Figure 5-2).

Facilitators schedule. Approximately three weeks before the actual conferences, students meet with their facilitators to schedule the conferences. Facilitators ask each child for a time that will work for his/her parents or guardians and schedule accordingly. If students are absent or unsure of a time that will work for their parent(s) or guardian, facilitators can simply select a time. Because a message on the postcard informs parents to call the school if the selected time does not work, this method avoids lengthy delays and rounds of "phone tag" trying to find a convenient time. We found a good rule of thumb was to schedule these "tentative" conference appointments for an evening slot. The final step is to fill in the correct time, date, and room on a postcard for each student; attach a mailing label; and return all postcards (along with the master schedules) to the office for mailing.

Schedule breaks. Facilitators were free to schedule themselves breaks during a conference time, but they were expected to be available in their rooms during the drop-in times. Because the student leads the conference, several conferences can occur simultaneously. We found it workable to schedule three conferences simultaneously during the day, and, if necessary, four during the evening session.

Figure 5-1 *Sample facilitator schedule*

MONDAY, NOV 22

Facilitator: _____   Conference Location _____

Time	Student Name	Parent/Guardian Name
7:30–8:00	_____	_____
7:30–8:00	_____	_____
7:30–8:00	_____	_____
8:00–8:30 (Drop-ins)	_____	
8:30–9:00	_____	_____
8:30–9:00	_____	_____
8:30–9:00	_____	_____
9:00–9:30 (Drop-ins)	_____	

Figure 5-2 *Sample postcards with schedules*

TALENT MIDDLE SCHOOL
STUDENT-LED CONFERENCES

Dear parents/guardians:

You and your child have been scheduled for a conference on:

_____ _____ _____
       (date)   (time)   (room)

_____ _____
      (student name)   (facilitator)

If you need to reschedule, please call Ms. Thiesen in Student Services at 535-XXXX.

If you wish to speak with specific teachers, a drop-in time will be available during the half-hour prior to and the half-hour following the scheduled conference. For those of you scheduled near a mealtime or at the end of the day, you may wish to call the school to confirm the availability of the drop-in time. Thank you!

TALENT MIDDLE SCHOOL
Conferencias dirigidas por los estudiantes

Estimados padres/representantes:

Se ha planeado una conferencia para Ud. y su hijo(a) el:

_____ _____ _____
       (fecha)   (hora)   (lugar)

_____ _____
      (nombre del estudiante)   (maestro supervisor)

Si usted necesita un día u hora diferente, favor llamar al 535-XXXX y pida hablar con Sra. Harlan (ella habla español). Si usted quisiera hablar con un maestro(a) específico, habrá un periodo de tiempo libre de 30 minutos antes y después de la conferencia elegida. Los que tienen una conferencia cerca de la hora de comer o al final del día, deben llamar a la escuela para confirmar esta cita. Gracias!

Collecting work samples

The first step in putting together the conference portfolio is for students to gather their work from all classes in one place. Designing a process that allows students to transport their work from their teachers to their conference facilitators will help this go smoothly. The school's collection process will depend somewhat on its organizational structure. If the school is organized by teams, students can simply take their work to the designated team member.

Another way is to give students a folder or a large sheet of paper folded in half during their first period classes. Students carry the folders with them during the day, adding work from each class. Five minutes before the end of the day, teachers dismiss students, who take their folders to their advisors. This can be done two days in a row for schools operating on a block schedule. We found that students were very responsible during this process and had only rare instances of work lost or misplaced during the day. On occasion, with a few high-needs students, teachers simply kept the work samples and placed them in the conference facilitator's box at the end of the day.

Organizing the work

A table of contents provides a consistent structure to help students organize their portfolios and allows parents to follow the presentation. To complete this step, students put their work in the order listed on the table of contents and wrote the name of the assignments in the appropriate places (see Figure 5-3).

Figure 5–3 *Sample portfolio table of contents*

Portfolio Table of Contents
Fall Student-Led Conferences

Name: __Elena__   Date: __October 26__

Dear Parent Letter
- Core (Reading, Writing, Social Studies) Cover Sheet
  - ABC book on elements: Devices
  - Personal narrative
  - Country study project
  - Essay on Honduras

- Mathematics Cover Sheet
  - Chapter test: Notes
  - Problem solving: Pizza Geometry

- Science or (Health) Cover Sheet
  - Literature circles: "The Accident"
  - Decision tree:

- Elective Cover Sheet
  - Band practice chart

- (PE) or Second Elective Cover Sheet
  - Fitness testing

- Report Card
- Goals for Success
- Parent Homework

Missing work

Each school must determine how to handle missing work. At TMS, we decided if a student took the initiative to find or complete the assignment, we would accept it for conference use. However, that did not mean the classroom teacher was required to accept it for full or even partial credit; that decision was left up to the teacher.

To indicate a piece of work was missing, we copied Figure 5-4 on astrobright pink paper. Students filled it out and put it in the place of any missing work. We found that students did not like to have this paper in their portfolios and would frequently finish or find the missing assignment. It wasn't unusual for a student to come running up to his facilitator to request immediate replacement of the missing work page with the actual completed assignment.

Figure 5–4 *Sample of completed Missing Work portfolio page*

Missing Work!

Name: Caroline   Teacher: Mrs. Monroe
Assignment Title: Character Report Card   Subject: Core
Assignment Due Date: 10-25-2012

I was given the opportunity to do this work but either did not complete it or turn it in because:

I swear I finished it. It just didn't make it to the school! First of all, my brother being such a klutz, spilt juice all over it. Trying to dry it off, I stuffed it in the dryer, which wasn't too smart. After going through 2 rolls of Scotch tape, I still couldn't get it into one piece, so I just gave up! I promise I'll turn it in next time!

Writing the "Dear Parent" letter

Remember the valuable lesson from Speech 101: the most difficult part of a presentation is getting started. By giving students a tool to use as an ice breaker, we set them up for success. Using a standard friendly letter format, students wrote a letter to their parent(s) or guardian(s) welcoming them to the conference, telling them about the contents of their portfolio, and explaining what they would share with them during the conference. Such letters may be creative, expressive, and personalized (see Figure 5-5 for a sample letter) or students can use a "fill in the blanks" template as a guide. Depending on how your school organizes conferences, the letter can be written under the direction of the conference facilitator, the student's language arts teacher, or another designee.

Figure 5-5 *Sample of Dear Parent letter*

Dear Mom,

Welcome to my mindblowing portfolio. You will be seeing my most magnificent work from various classes. These classes are Science, Math, Band, Core, and P.E. I'm really excited that you will get to see my divine piece of writing that I did in Core.

My greatest strength is that I work independently. My greatest weakness is I don't always get my work in on time.

Thank you for coming. I hope you learn from all this that I work really hard.

Love,
Galen

Goal setting

Once students have organized their work and written their "Dear Parent" letters, they will review their work as they begin the goal-setting process. Please refer to Chapter 6 for more information on this part of the process.

Teaching the process

Helping students see the overall process they will follow sets the stage for a successful conference. Depending on the age and maturity of the students involved, the process may be a general outline for them to follow or a more detailed "fill in the blanks" script. At TMS, we taught our students to use the following steps to guide their SLC:

- Introduce your parents to your advisor.

- Explain that you be will sharing work collected from the first 12 weeks of school.

- Briefly review the Table of Contents to give your parents an overview of what is inside your portfolio.

- Read aloud your "Dear Parent" letter.

- Present your work following the order in the Table of Contents.

- For each subject:
  - Explain the cover sheet, how you scored your work, and how your teacher scored your work.
  - Share the work sample(s).
    - Explain what knowledge and skills you learned using examples from your work.
    - Share the process you used to complete and evaluate the assignment.
    - Read aloud key portions of your self-reflections.

- Share your report card

- Explain the two goals you have set.

- Write the third goal with your parents.

- Explain to your parents what they need to do for the Parent Homework Letter.

- Thank your parents for coming.

- Use the drop-in time to visit any teacher with whom your
  parents would like to chat.

Some schools prefer to use a more structured approach for their conference
scripts. A partial example of a "fill in the blanks" script is as follows:

- I'd like to start by sharing my language arts folder with you. The first
  piece I will talk about is a persuasive essay I wrote a few weeks ago.
  In it, I am trying to persuade someone that _____.

- Here is the introductory paragraph. (Share opening paragraph).

- This is a good example of a persuasive essay because _____.

- I (do/do not) have trouble with writing persuasive essays because

  _____

- One area of writing that I can improve is _____.

- I believe I (do/do not do) my best in writing because _____.

Sharing the report card

Depending on the timing of your SLCs, you may or may not have a report card
to share with the parents. Because our conferences were at the end of the
first trimester, we chose to include the report card in the conference portfolio.
We deliberately placed it at the end of the portfolio, just before the goal
setting. Because the students were so thorough in sharing their work during
the conference, by the time they presented the report card, there were very
few questions about the grades students earned.

Parent homework (optional)

Middle school students love the idea of giving their parents a homework
assignment. Because one of the goals of a student-led conference is to
foster better communication between students and parents regarding
progress in school, we created the parent homework assignment. At the
end of the conference, students give their parents an assignment sheet
(Figure 5-6) asking them to respond to the conference in writing. This optional

"assignment" may or may not be returned to the teacher. The responses often are very touching and meaningful to the student.

Figure 5-6 *Sample parent homework*

Parent Homework
Dear Parent,
THANK YOU for participating in your child's conference .... now you have some homework. Please write your child a positive personal note about the conference. Below are some areas you might think about including as you write:
• What I noticed about your work was …   • I was proud of you for …   • Keep up the good work on …   • I know you have difficulty sometimes, but …   • I'm glad you are making an extra effort in …   • How can I help you?
We hope this experience was as rewarding to you and your child as the process was to us. Thanks again for taking the extra effort!
Sincerely,   Talent Middle School Staff

Practicing the presentation

Once students understand the steps they will follow for the conference, it's time to practice. A good way to begin is to show a video of a student giving a portion of a student-led conference (this can be of an actual conference or one that has been created for this purpose). You might also begin the practice session by having a capable student present the portfolio to the facilitator in front of the class. A variation on this is to have multiple students present the portfolio to the group, each person doing a different section of the conference. Because our conference groups were multi-graded, it was always possible to use the more experienced 8th graders to demonstrate the process for the others.

Working in pairs seems to be the most effective way for students to practice for the conference. Emphasize creating a smooth presentation that flows easily from one section to another; remember, students have already had the opportunity to practice their pieces separately in their subject area classes. Students can take turns presenting their portfolios to each other. For the first practice session, if possible, pair up any student new to SLCs with a partner who has done one in the past. Changing groups for subsequent practice sessions keeps students' interest at a higher level.

How long does this process take? We generally scheduled four or five days of 35-minute sessions for the students to work with their facilitators on portfolio organization, goal setting, and practicing the conference presentation. At the end of practice sessions, students fill out a final invitation (Figure 5-7) to take home as a reminder for the conference, and then they are ready for the next step—successfully leading the conference.

Figure 5-7 *Sample postcard reminder of conference date and time*

You're invited to…

my student-led conference at Talent Middle School!

I've been working hard to get ready to share my school work with you.

Please come next week and enjoy seeing what I've done.

Thank you!

Our conference is scheduled

Date: _____

Time: _____

Room: _____

Facilitator: _____

 Chapter 6

Setting Goals for the Future

Portfolios and student-led conferences are part of a larger purpose: improving student learning. Crucial to achieving this outcome is the goal-setting process. This step provides an opportunity for students to analyze their strengths and growth areas and develop an improvement plan that empowers them to take charge of their own learning. However, to be truly effective, goal setting must be done in a supportive environment, and using SLCs to make goal setting a joint venture involving students, families, and the school leads to strong connections between home and school.

A TMS parent agrees. When asked what she liked best about SLCs, she responded:

> You involve your child with the goals. They get to be involved
> rather than a teacher or parent talking about what they want
> for the child; you bring the child into the whole process. When
> they're setting goals for themselves, they are more apt to keep
> the goals. They are also setting them with the people who are
> there to help them accomplish those goals. It's important to
> the student and important to the teachers also. He's able to
> see his strengths and weaknesses, and he's held accountable
> by the people who are there to help him improve and do better.
> He sees his own strengths and weaknesses and is able to
> see where he is now and where he needs to be by the end of
> the year and where he needs to be in his life. I think that's the
> best thing.

Goal setting must be designed to help students develop clear, specific, doable steps to succeed as learners. In our SLC model there are three steps to this process: setting preliminary goals before the conference, sharing the goals during the conference (including creating one in collaboration with parents), and finally, revisiting goals regularly to assess and revise for further success.

Step One: Setting goals before the conference.

To begin the goal-setting process, students use knowledge gained through the self-reflection process to choose three strengths and three areas for improvement. Most students find this process easy, but if students struggle with this, have them re-read their self-reflections and identify strengths and areas of growth that may have been suggested. From this information students then choose three areas to develop goals.

Encourage students to select a mix of academic and behavioral goals because it is often a behavior that keeps some students from being successful. For example, procrastination and talking in class are two areas with which many middle schoolers struggle. We found that students who have reflected on their work in a thoughtful manner often arrive at the goals we would have chosen for them—but there is a much higher likelihood of success when they are the ones to recognize and set an improvement goal in those areas.

Students often struggle more with determining specific actions necessary to achieve their goals. Teachers can assist students in breaking the goal into clear, measurable steps by first asking them to think of a general goal, for example, "I want to write better." Next, help them clarify that goal by asking them to determine a specific skill or behavior that will help them "write better." For example, "I need to work on writing sentences that flow and sound natural when read aloud." The students then decide on two things that they can do to accomplish that goal. For instance, a student might (1) ask another student or the computer to read his paper aloud so he can listen to the flow of his writing, and (2) read the paper aloud to parents or a friend and ask them to listen to the flow of the sentences.

Also helpful is to show students what former students have used as goals and actions. To do this, we compiled a list of student-created goals and action plans from previous goal sheets and used them as exemplars (see Figure 6-1).

Figure 6-1 *Examples of goals and specific actions to accomplish them*

Sample Goals and Action Plans

Goal: Work on not procrastinating
Action Plan:

- Make a plan; post due dates on refrigerator
- Work on homework before turning on TV
- Do homework right away—not at last minute
- Plan my days better
- Stop putting things off

Goal: Control my talking in class
Action Plan:

- Sit with people I won't talk to
- Focus on my work
- Tell my friends ahead of time
- Don't talk back when friends talk to me
- Explain to friends I'm not being rude—I'm trying to accomplish my goal
- Stay in my seat
- Mind my own business

Goal: Bring my practice chart to band
Action Plan:

- Have my mom and dad sign my practice chart
- Practice more
- Get my mom to sign the chart 1 day early

Goal: Be more consistent with commitments
Action Plan:

- Stay focused on my work and work until it's done
- Try hard in class and leave reminders for myself

Goal: Get my math homework done
Action Plan:

- Set aside 15 minutes to get homework done
- Try not to talk so much in class

Goal: Better my attendance
Action Plan:

- Get a flu shot
- Get more rest
- Avoid staying out so late

Goal: Improve responses to reading
Action Plan:

- Think before I write
- Better understand the reading scoring guide

Goal: Interact better with people/Manage my emotions more positively
Action Plan:

- Talk with mom and dad about anger
- Identify my anger and get advice on how to deal with it
- Listen to other people's ways; find common ground

Goal: Read every day
Action Plan:

- See media specialist for new books
- Read at night before I go to bed
- Read 4 nights a week for 20–30 minutes
- Remember to bring my book to school so I can read during silent reading

Goal: Improve scores on problem solving in math
Action Plan:

- Put more time into the work
- Study and understand the math scoring guide
- Explain all my ideas clearly

Goal: Remember to study for tests
Action Plan:

- Write myself a note with everything the test will cover
- Study for at least 20 minutes a night
- Put notes in my math text as a reminder

Goal: Get more active in what my class is doing
Action Plan:

- Ask questions about assigned problems
- Try to understand the problem and how to solve it

Goal: Get along with my math teacher and work harder in class
Action Plan:

- Work on my attitude
- Do my work without saying anything

Goal: Keep track of my papers so I'll have what I need when I need it
Action Plan:

- Remember where I put everything I need
- Stick with my new system of using 2 binders (one for every 2-3 classes)

Goal: Improve my speaking in front of the class
Action Plan:

- Practice my speech
- Write out speech and plan

Goal: Write my due dates in my planning calendar and check it daily
Action Plan:

- Record my assignments when I get them
- Check my calendar daily

Goal: Reduce time spent on electronics for fun
Action Plan:

- Limit to ½ hour per evening on weeknights
- Limit to 2 hours per day on weekends

Asking students to write goals increases the chances of their working to meet the goals. Reading the goals aloud to a significant person further increases this likelihood. We ask students to choose two goals to write on the goal form and to keep the third goal in abeyance until the actual conference when they can use it as the backup for setting a joint goal with parents. The final pre-conference goal step is to list people who can help with attaining the goals and noting distractions that may inhibit success.

Step Two: Sharing the goals

Prior to sharing goals during the conference, students show work from all classes and discuss the skills, processes, and content learned. They also share key points from the self-reflections that lead naturally into the goal-setting part of the conference. At that time the conference facilitator rejoins the discussion to become part of the goal-setting team. Remaining in the background prior to this time, the conference facilitator has allowed the conversation to develop between students and parents. We discovered that when the facilitator stays at the table for the entire conference, parents more often direct the questions and comments to the adult. However, with younger students, the teacher may want to provide additional support by staying at the table, while ensuring that the student is in charge of leading the conversation.

The student begins by sharing strengths and areas for improvement. From there, the student shares the first two goals along with the plan for action. The student invites parents to help refine the goals and action plan if necessary. Collaborating on the third goal starts with the student asking whether the parents have a third goal in mind. If they draw a blank, the student brings the "backup goal" up for discussion. Together, they create and write an action plan (see Figure 6-2). Parents then review the list of helpers and distractions the student created earlier and suggest any additions.

Figure 6-2 *Sample goals from a student-led conference*

Goals for Success

Name: Michael   Date: 11/19/12

My strengths are:

   A. Being descriptive in my writings.

   B. Getting work done on time in Science.

   C. Turning in my practice chart on time in Band.

I need to work on:

   A. Not socializing with my friends during class.

   B. Using teamwork in P.E.

   C. Cooperating with my lab partners.

First Goal: Not to socialize with my friends when I'm not allowed to. To achieve this goal, I will

   A. Sit by people I won't talk to.

   B. Ignore them if they talk to me.

Second Goal: I will try to cooperate with the partner I'm assigned to. To achieve this goal, I will

   A. I will let them try the stuff I would want to try.

   B. I will try to get better at getting along with different people.

Third Goal: If I don't understand my work, I will get help instead of skipping it. To achieve this goal, I will

   A. Ask other students or my parents for help.

   B. Ask the teacher to help me.

   C. Try to explain it to someone else.

People who can help me attain these goals are:

Mom, teachers, friends, and myself.

Distractions that may get in the way of accomplishing these goals are:

TV, my sister, and friends.

Michael	Valerie Smith	Patti Kinney
Student Signature	Parent Signature	Facilitator

By signing the goal sheet, all members of the team make a commitment to help the student work toward success, and the family takes a signed copy home to place in a prominent spot—possibly the refrigerator door; the conference facilitator keeps another copy at school.

Step Three: Revisiting goals

Accountability is important in achieving goals. Set dates for periodic reviews of progress—both at home and in school—to accomplish the previously agreed upon goals. Reviews at home are less formal, but they do provide students and their parents a chance to revisit the goals and discuss progress toward meeting the goals. By revisiting their goals with teachers and/or parents, students develop the skills and knowledge to successfully reach their goals and set new ones.

At progress report time (midway through the next trimester), our students meet again with their conference facilitator. Together, they review the original goal sheets, and on a goals-revisited form (see Figure 6-3), students indicate progress (or lack of it). If necessary, the action plan is refined or changed to help students continue to make progress. If a goal has already been achieved, they identify a new goal. The original copy of the goals-revisited page is then sent home along with the student's progress report, and the conference facilitator keeps the other copy. This revisiting process holds students accountable for monitoring their own progress on a regular basis.

We have found that goal setting is an important piece of the conference process and helps students learn to accept responsibility for their own learning and growth. Psychologist Mihalyi Czikszentmikaly (1990) made an interesting discovery about the connection between goals and happiness: "Goals are the stuff of motivation, persistence and well-being." He discovered that what people enjoy most is pursuing a clear, doable goal that they value. Goals are essential to student improvement.

Figure 6-3 *Sample revisiting goals from student-led conference*

Goals for Success: Revisited

Name: Michael   Date: 1/23/12

First Goal: Not to socialize with my friends when I'm not allowed to.

List two things you have done (or are doing) to meet this goal.

    A. I am sitting by people I won't talk to.

    B. I am ignoring people that do talk to me.

What are two things you can do (or continue to do) in the next few weeks to make sure you are successful in meeting this goal?

    A. I can ask the teacher to help me sit in a good place.

    B. I can ignore people that try to talk to me.

Circle the word that describes your effort to date in meeting Goal 1:

None   Little   Some   (Good)   Excellent

Second Goal: I will try to cooperate with the partner I'm assigned to.

List two things you have done (or are doing) to meet this goal.

    A. I will try to let them do stuff that I would want to do.

    B. I am trying to get better at getting along with different people.

What are two things you can do (or continue to do) in the next few weeks to make sure you are successful in meeting this goal?

    A. I am continuing to get along with different people.

    B. I will try to let them do stuff I would want to do.

Circle the word that describes your effort to date in meeting Goal 2:

None   Little   (Some)   Good   Excellent

Third Goal: If I don't understand my work, I will get help instead of skipping it.

List two things you have done (or are doing) to meet this goal.

    A. Asked for help.

    B. Asked the teacher to help me.

What are two things you can do (or continue to do) in the next few weeks to make sure you are successful in meeting this goal?

    A. Ask for help.

    B. Try to explain it to someone else.

Circle the word that describes your effort to date in meeting Goal 3:

None   Little   (Some)   Good   Excellent

Chapter 7

The Conference

Conference day has arrived. As students and their parents or guardians walk down the hallway, you can almost hear the wheels turning as students run through a final practice in their minds. The classroom they enter has been organized to accommodate up to four simultaneous conferences. The arrangement of chairs and tables allows for maximum privacy.

Lane: Mom and Dad, I would like you to meet my teacher, Mrs. Munroe. Mrs. Munroe, these are my parents, Teresa and Mike.

Mrs.Munroe: I'm glad you're here. It's nice to meet you. If you'd come over here, we have the conference all set up so we can get started. Lane, if you'll sit in the middle, I'll explain how this conference is going to work, as it may be a bit different than other conferences you've attended.

Lane has been practicing what he's going to say, and he's going to be sharing his work with you, what he believes he's good at, and what he needs to improve. I'll be in the room and come back near the end when he's ready to share his goals, so I can listen in and help him achieve his goals, too. Other than that, he's the one running the conference.

At this point the parents and their child sit together at a table. The student is in the center; adult(s), on either side. The portfolio is ready and waiting on the table. The teacher fades into the background and lets the student take over.

Dad: Sounds good. Are you ready?

Lane: No (with a laugh) but here goes. Mom, Dad, this is my portfolio, and I'll start with this that I have written to you guys to introduce you to my portfolio.

Figure 7-1 *Letter to parents that starts conference*

Dear Mom and Dad,

Whew, the trimester is almost over, and yes, I have learned a lot. This portfolio has some of my best work (even though I only have best work). I hope you enjoy seeing my growth through this trimester, and I can even see some improvement in my own work. My favorite piece in this folder is my descriptive writing that you will soon see. I've seen growth in my schoolwork, and I hope you do too.

If you have any special questions for any of my Teachers, you can stop by their rooms and visit with them during the drop-in period.

Love,
your son Lane

Mom: Great!

The "Dear Parent letter" has served its purpose. The ice is broken and the conference is off to a good start.

Lane: This is my reading list and these are the books that I've read this trimester.

Dad: What does this number mean?

Lane: It's the rating for the different types of books. You rate the book between 1 and 5 to show how much you liked it. And then…

Mom: So this one that's got a 6++ must mean you really liked it.

Lane: Yeah, I really loved that one.

Dad: So, that doesn't necessarily indicate how difficult it is to read.

Lane: No, that's here. Difficulty is easy, average, hard.

Dad: Oh, I see.

Lane: This is one of my first responses for this year, and I feel it is one of my best. It shows that I can evaluate and predict, and I did pretty good on it.

Mom: Can I ask a question? In response to what?

Lane: It's a response to a book that I read during that day.

Mom: Oh, okay.

Lane: Like what you read about—if you see any connections between your life and what the character or someone in the book is feeling.

Mom: Sort of like a daily journal?

Lane: Yeah. This is my book project on Gary Paulsen. I figured out this year that I liked him a lot—his style of adventure. He's not just a phony writer; it could be reality—and most things are based on his experience. This is my reading self-evaluation. The number of novels I've read so far this year is five, and two of the ones I liked a lot are *The Foxman* by Gary Paulsen and *The Voyage of the Frog*. I'm not sure at this moment who wrote that one.

Mom: This is the one you had as a 6++.

The conference continues as Lane moves into a section on social studies. He shows his parents the work he has completed while studying ancient Greece and concludes by summarizing his accomplishments.

Lane: These are my requirements that I fulfilled during this project on ancient Greece. Some of the things I did were communicated through writing, speaking, and visual forms, and some other stuff. I've been a self-directed learner by trying to stay focused. I've used technology and computers and some other things. I've also shown I'm able to interpret literature.

In Lane's conference, work from his health class comes next.

Lane: This is my book we had to write for health about alcohol and what can happen if you use it. I wrote a "choose your own adventure" book.

Mom: I remember when you worked on that.

Lane: Yeah, you guys helped on this. It tells about the kind of choices you can make, like if you accept a drink of alcohol or not...the reflection asked "what was the hardest part of the project?" and I wrote, "Making up the story because I had a hard time deciding on what to write and how to say it." And for "If I could do this project again, what would I do differently?" I wrote, "I'd change it to an alphabet style book, like A is for alcohol, B is for booze, and have little stick figures doing something to illustrate each letter."

Mom: Well, I like the way you did it!

The math section begins with an explanation of the cover sheet.

Lane: This is my math section and my teacher is Mrs. Bostwick and I'm in pre-algebra. For having materials in class and being ready to work, I gave myself a check plus and she scored me a plus.

Dad: Good

Lane: For "Is responsible for assigned tasks" we both marked a check. For "makes a positive contribution to class" we both marked a plus, and she commented "Lane is a good student and does well in math."

Mom: Thanks to his dad!! (laughter)

An in-depth conversation about his math work is followed by a discussion of what has been happening in physical education.

Lane: In PE we did a self-reflection on the trimester. We had to choose an activity that we did and explain three rules. I chose basketball and the rules are… Then we had to tell if we followed the rules honestly and I put "mostly" because sometimes I tend to foul a little bit, but sometimes that's expected!

Mom: Sounds like something you can work on.

Lane: This is my "missing work" page because I didn't do my make-ups when I had a dentist appointment a while back.

Mom: How does that affect your PE grade?

Lane: I lose 5 points off my total for each make-up I don't turn in. It won't matter much 'cause I only did it once. So I'm fine.

At this point the conference moves into goal setting and Mrs. Munroe joins the group. Prior to this, she has worked quietly in the room, helped another conference group get started, and finished a discussion of goals with another student.

Lane: My strengths are that I understand math concepts pretty well, I can read fast, have a good vocabulary, and I can follow directions well. What I need to work on are spelling words, talking too much, and waking up on time! My first goal is that I will not be as social in class. To achieve this goal, I will be quiet when I'm told to, listen well, and look at the teacher to show I am paying attention. My second goal is that I will watch TV one hour or less on weekdays—I want to cut my watching time. To achieve this goal, I'll read more in my spare time and participate in more sport activities.

MAYBE ONLY 2 goals or class on 1 cristted out 7 of 1 ended

Dad: I'd like to comment that I think you're already working on and making good progress with this goal. You have increased your reading three- or four-fold—and it's making a difference.

Lane: I need your help in writing a third goal. Do you have any ideas?

Silence for a few moments.

Mrs. Munroe: You've looked at his work and you've seen him at home. He's shared goals he feels are important and he has an idea for a third, but is there one that you feel would help him not only be a better student but learn something you feel is important for him to know?

Mom: One that is more life skills than academic is dealing with anger management—finding healthier ways to vent teen frustrations.

Lane: How could I write that—manage my anger?

Mom: Maybe handle your emotions in a positive manner.

Mrs. Munroe: So how could you do that?

Lane: Well, I already do sports and that helps me work out some of my feelings.

Mom: How about identify the source of anger or frustration? That way you put it in its proper place rather than take it out on someone else.

Mrs. Munroe: Does that make sense to you?

Lane: Not really.

Mrs. Munroe: It sounds like she's saying you tend to react to outside things. It's like I go home and I kick the dog, but I'm not really angry at the dog.

Mom: Yeah, you come home from school and something has happened and you take it out on all of us by yelling and being in a bad mood.

Lane: Okay, that makes sense to me. People who can help me are family, friends, and teachers.

Dad: What will get in your way?

Lane: Maybe watching too much TV or spending time on the computer.

The conference wraps up a few minutes later when Lane explains the parent homework assignment to his mother and father. He hands his parents an evaluation form and asks them to turn it in near the school entrance. As they leave the room, they say good-bye and decide which teachers they should visit during the drop-in time.

 Chapter 8

Wrap Up

Think back to the steps of the process circle that was shared in the beginning of the book (Figure 2-1). To ensure lasting and future success with the conferences, you must monitor and adjust the process. Too many times a good idea has been tried and rejected outright because it "didn't work" as well as was hoped. Instead, begin the process with the mindset that it will only get better with time and plan upfront how you will monitor the process, gather feedback from all stakeholders, and make adjustments based on the data collected.

Staff feedback

It is critical that the teachers in your school feel that their concerns are heard. If your school is like ours, likely you will not have 100 percent, enthusiastic buy-in for your first attempt at SLCs. Change can be difficult for many, and stepping outside comfort zones can be troubling. Ask staff for feedback in writing (see Figure 8-1) and analyze it carefully. Often, a few minor adjustments in the logistics have a tremendous impact on your colleagues' perceptions of the process.

Figure 8-1 *Sample staff evaluation form*

Staff Evaluation of Student-Led Conferences

We would like everybody to complete this form in the next few days.
By Thursday, please put the completed form in the envelope in the office
and check off your name.

How many years have you facilitated SLCs?

❑ 1   ❑ 2   ❑ 3   ❑ 4   ❑ 5 or more

Using a scale of 1 *(poor)*, 2 *(okay)*, 3 *(fine)*, 4 *(good)*, 5 *(very good)*, 6 *(excellent)*,
how would you rate the overall process and format?

1   2   3   4   5   6

Please indicate your thoughts on the following areas. If you indicate "needs work,"
please give details and suggestions for improvement.

1. Your knowledge of process (knew expectations, dates, process, etc.)
❑ no problems
❑ needs work

2. Preparation of student work in the classroom (knew expectations, due dates, etc.)
❑ no problems
❑ needs work

3. Scheduling process (office does families, facilitators do postcards, etc.)
❑ no problems
❑ needs work

4. Schedule used (times, drop-ins, evening schedule, schedule own breaks, etc.)
❑ no problems
❑ needs work

5. Collection of work (use of paper folder, students collect work over two days, etc.)
❑ no problems
❑ needs work

6. Table of Contents and "Dear Parent" Letter (Facilitators responsible for helping students organize and get the table of contents filled out; core teachers have students write letter.)

❏ no problems
❏ needs work

7. Writing of goals
❏ no problems
❏ needs work

8. Process for practicing with facilitators (amount of time, use of video, etc.)
❏ no problems
❏ needs work

9. Notification of changes in conference schedule
❏ no problems
❏ needs work

10. Other: Please comment on any area not addressed above. Thanks!

Parent feedback

Feedback received from parents can also be very beneficial for improving the process. Because parents have not been as involved in creating and implementing the process as staff and students, they will look at it from a different perspective and often provide feedback and suggestions that can greatly improve the process. The first year we implemented SLCs, every parent completed an evaluation form (Figure 8-2) at the end of the conference and turned it in as they left the building. Although overall the comments were extremely positive, we learned there were areas about which we had not given sufficient clear information. For example, many parents seemed confused about the purpose of the drop-in visits, with several expressing disappointment about not getting time to speak with their child's teacher.

The following year, we addressed this by ensuring that information about drop-in opportunities was published in the school newsletter and written on the post cards mailed home to confirm the conference appointment. Subsequently, drop-in time was more effective and caused less concern. As parents became more familiar with the process, we found it unnecessary to have every parent fill out an evaluation form every year. Some years, instead of giving every parent the form at the end of each conference, we simply had them available near the front door.

Figure 8-2 *Sample parent evaluation form*

Parent Evaluation of Student-Led Conferences

Parents,
Thank you for coming. We hope you enjoyed your visit. Please take
a moment to answer the following questions before you leave.
TMS Staff

Please circle the number that corresponds to whether you agree/disagree
with the statement.

1. My child was prepared for the conference.

Strongly disagree   Strongly agree
    1   2   3   4   5

2. I now have a better understanding of how my child learns.

Strongly disagree   Strongly agree
    1   2   3   4   5

3. I have a clear picture about what my child has been studying this trimester.

Strongly disagree   Strongly agree
    1   2   3   4   5

4. I have a better understanding of my child's effort, study skills,
and classroom behaviors.

Strongly disagree   Strongly agree
    1   2   3   4   5

5. The student-led conference was valuable and informative.

Strongly disagree   Strongly agree
    1   2   3   4   5

6. My child wrote goals that will help improve his/her performance.

Strongly disagree   Strongly agree
    1   2   3   4   5

7. Additional Comments:

Student feedback

Middle school students can be brutally honest and are quite willing to give their opinions when asked. In our first few years of SLCs, we asked all students to give us written feedback about the process (see Figure 8-3). However, experience taught us that we get similar information, with less resistance, if we simply hold a class discussion about what went well and what didn't go as well. This discussion worked fine when combined with a celebration complete with treats.

Figure 8-3 *Sample questions for student feedback (written or discussion)*

Post-Conference Thoughts
Things went smoothly during the conference because…   Things could have gone better if…   One thing I wish I would have shared with my parents, but forgot is…   One thing I chose not to share, but should have…   The best thing about this experience was…   Anything else??

Making adjustments

After all the feedback has been compiled and analyzed, it's time to make decisions on necessary revisions for the next time. Don't put this off until later; it's much more effective while the conferences are fresh on everyone's mind, and people remember why they felt something did or did not work. An effective strategy is to create a small committee with representatives from all content areas or teams. Have this group carefully analyze the feedback data and differentiate consistent trends from isolated concerns. Then decide which issues realistically can be handled and plan the appropriate adjustments.

In addition to making adjustments to the overall process, you might consider providing additional services for your students and parents. During the evening conference times, the PTA or another group could provide dinner at a reasonable cost; supervised childcare is another popular feature.

Even after conducting SLCs for nearly twenty years, TMS continues to add new features to their conferences. This past year, during the busy evening times, informational tables for parents and students were set up in an open area; numerous agencies, colleges, and community programs provided information. Parents and students visited the area before or after the conferences to talk with providers and gather information about: the district high school and its programs; local health and human services that help families; after school programs for middle level students; state colleges/ universities, the local community college, and more. The goal was to provide parents resources to help them face the constant learning curve of raising adolescents and to get them thinking about high school and college opportunities and challenges.

For SLCs to be successful, evaluation must be an ongoing process. Yearly evaluations to determine what needs to be refined are critical. These adjustments will help you adapt the process to fit your school and thus help you better meet the often-changing needs of the students and community you serve.

And, finally, don't forget to celebrate!

Everyone needs to give themselves a pat on the back and celebrate because putting together a successful round of SLCs is hard work and deserves recognition. Acknowledge staff contributions to the process, bring in treats, have a social time, and just relax when it's all over.

Also, the students deserve recognition for their efforts. After fall SLCs, we would generally bring in treats for all students and let them know we appreciated their hard work in preparing for and leading the conferences.

In the spring, when our 8th graders finished their benchmark presentations (a more formalized version of SLCs in which they share their academic growth during middle school and their progress toward meeting state standards), all students who completed their presentations were taken on a field trip or to a special activity arranged just for them.

Chapter 9

Going It Alone: An Individual or Team Approach

The initial implementation of student-led conferences at TMS began with a grassroots effort by two teachers. Their early work gained momentum until the process was adapted and implemented on a school-wide basis. For individuals or teams ready to try student-led conferences, but who do not yet have the support or resources to begin a school-wide initiative, here is a story of a successful implementation by a middle school team.

"We're Making it Work"

Student-Led Conferences in Action: A Team Approach

Theresa Hinkle, teacher (retired),
John R. Kernodle Middle School,
Greensboro, NC

"Why did you give me that grade?"
"I turned that work in!"
"How did I get a "C"?"

"I just missed a few homework assignments; I can't believe they counted that much!"
"Susie says she doesn't have any idea what she could have done to earn a better grade."

If any of these statements sound familiar, you might be dealing with the same dilemma my team faced. For years we wrestled with the question of how an interdisciplinary team could help students acquire the skills and knowledge to take ownership for their learning. In addition, we wanted this process to include giving students the responsibility for both informing parents of progress and setting goals for improvement.

Our quest to find solutions led me to a session on SLCs at a state middle school conference. Inspired by the success stories and how-to handout of an enthusiastic team from a nearby city, as well as support and resources from TMS, I was able to get my team started.

As with any borrowed idea, my team set out to make the process our own. We quickly realized we would face scheduling challenges because we were the only team implementing SLCs. Secondly, we examined the various methods one might use for preparing students for the conferences and debated which would best serve our students. Finally, we decided upon the logistics of how our team could best implement the process.

Scheduling

Scheduling was the primary reason I had previously dropped the idea of implementing SLCs. Without a supportive school schedule, I was concerned that it would be too cumbersome to implement. To create our schedule, we recognized that the conferences needed to be held at a variety of times to meet the work schedules of our parents, and we had to consider where and when space was available. We determined that before-school conferences and conferences held during our planning periods would take place in our classrooms. This still left the dilemma of a location for conferences held at times during the day when we were teaching. It was time to ask for support, so we enlisted administrators, our guidance counselor, and two elective teachers who served as advisors on our team. Each agreed to help supervise conferences held in the school cafeteria and media center throughout the day.

Preparing students

Next we had to decide how best to prepare our students to conduct a SLC. Our team regularly posted grade sheets, so students could keep up with missing work, averages, etc. Because this wasn't working for all our students, we decided to add the additional layer of subject portfolios. We felt these portfolios would be an invaluable resource as students prepared for their conferences. We made decisions about how to organize the portfolios, and we scheduled occasional advisory periods for portfolio, review and maintenance. One of our most helpful strategies was to require students to fill out brightly colored forms each time an assignment was not turned in on time. If the work was turned in late (yes, we accepted late work with certain conditions), we attached it to the brightly colored "missing work" forms. These forms were easy for parents to spot and led to interesting conversations between parents and students.

While we hoped this portfolio system would provide adequate information for parents, we also examined our system for distributing interim reports that were sent home every four to five weeks. The usual pattern was that as soon as they received the reports, parents would write or call to inquire about missing work, low grades, etc. Our typical reply of, "Did you ask your child?" was usually met with a "he/she doesn't know." This was definitely an area of concern for the team, so we addressed the problem in the following manner:

- The day before interims were sent home, we distributed them to students the last 10 minutes of class.

- Students compared the posted grades with those in their work portfolios and reported any discrepancies to the teacher. Clerical errors were corrected and revised reports printed.

- Students wrote a brief note on the interim to their parents explaining their grades, pointing out their successes and acknowledging their areas of weakness. Many students ended these notes with promises of doing better.

- The interims were collected and redistributed the next day. Students especially liked knowing the grades they would be taking home the next day.

The results were astounding. With only a couple exceptions, the messages we received from parents were notes of thanks. Many parents said this was the first time their child had been able to explain his or her grades and that the notes opened the door for great conversations. This knowledge of progress and ability to communicate with parents about their work was a huge step for our students.

Logistical planning

At this point we felt we were on the right track and got down to the nuts and bolts of planning our first student-led conferences. We found many of the forms and suggestions in *A School-Wide Approach to Student-Led Conferences* (2000) suited our needs well, and we used them for scheduling, planning, and follow-up. We decided that our seventh graders would not need a scripted conference, so we created a general outline for them to follow when presenting their portfolio.

Conference day

The day of conferences arrived with over 90% of our parents scheduled to conference with their children. The before-school conferences went well with teachers floating from classroom to classroom simply to provide a presence…the students were doing all the work. They were excited about their responsibilities and took them very seriously. We were all a little anxious about the conferences being held during the time we were in class. We had considered consolidating classes, so one of the core teachers would be free but had decided against that approach because we had the support of our administrators and others who had agreed to float through the cafeteria and media center throughout the day.

Things seemed to be running smoothly. Two students were manning a check-in desk at the front door of the school; when parents entered, these greeters escorted them to the classroom where they met their child and proceeded to the location of the conference. Students were quietly slipping in and out of the room as their conferences started and ended. I was feeling much better until I looked up to see my principal standing in the doorway motioning for me to come into the hall. Fearing the worst, I stepped out to find him beaming as he said, "This is the most exciting thing I've seen in years. You just have to walk through the cafeteria and see what is happening." It was wonderful...students and parents pouring over work, students leading the conversation about their grades and efforts, collaborative goal setting, meaningful dialogue about school and grades...and not a teacher in sight. The feedback gathered from parents immediately after the conferences was very positive, but perhaps the most meaningful feedback came in the letters parents wrote to their children.

If I were asked if I recommend whole-school implementation of student-led conferencing, I would reply, "Absolutely." But if that isn't possible, implementation of this powerful protocol by even a single teacher or team can and will make a difference for the students they teach. These conferences are a powerful tool that helps students think about their learning, communicate with parents, and assume responsibility for their educations.

Chapter 10

Taking it to the Elementary and High School Levels

Student-led conferences can be successfully implemented for any grade level by making adaptations based on student age, abilities, and the amount of adult support needed. Below are examples of how an elementary school and a high school have adapted the process to work in their settings.

Student-Led Conferences in Action: It's Elementary

Kristin Nori, Elementary Teacher, Charlotte, NC

I still can't believe the families of all twenty-one of my fifth graders came the first year I held true student-led conferences. I remember being told to prepare myself for low attendance as many of the parents in this lower socioeconomic neighborhood would not have the time or care enough to come in. It was the fall of 2007, and I was teaching fifth grade in Maryland in a school that did not quite qualify for Title I services, yet had many students who lived well below the poverty line. A significant number spoke English as their second language and had moved frequently in their short lives. The parents of these students were extremely young, worked in "no work, no pay" blue-collar jobs and viewed parent-teacher conferences as unimportant. I knew if I wanted the families of my students to attend their conference,

I would have to be creative and think outside the box to make that happen.

I had had some training on how to hold student-led conferences, so I decided to hold them with the hope that the students themselves would encourage their families to attend. I presented the idea, trained the class, and set up my appointments. I know it sounds like it just happened, but it really did. They all came. If a student could not get a parent to come, they brought an older sibling, aunt, mentor, babysitter, or family friend. In one case, the student's mother did not speak English, so she brought her older sister to help with translating. But in the end, every last one of my students conducted their first student-led conference.

Before conference day

I began by sharing my expectations with the students and explained to them they were going to present their data notebooks and their grades to their parents. The students already kept a data notebook of common assessment scores, reading, math, and spelling grades, as well as their educational goals.

At the beginning of the term, I taught the students how to set specific quarterly goals. For example, rather than just stating "Get an A in math", the student would write, "Earn 93% or higher on all tests and class work grades in math to earn an A for the term." Students then created an action plan for the next marking period. Based on their grades, students picked an area or two of focus and explained why the score was lower than they would like. They next developed at least three strategies for improvement during the following quarter. This became one of the main talking points at the conference.

Finally, students picked a piece of creative writing to share and were taught how to explain the writing process and how they created the story they wrote.

Conference day

The conference began when the parents arrived, and I explained that their child was going to present the information as well as the action plan we had worked together to create. I emphasized the student was in charge, and they should direct their questions to their child. At first, it was hard for the parents because they had never experienced student-led conferences. However, I found the parents became very supportive of this process.

The student then took the lead and began by sharing the report card. They then discussed strengths and weaknesses and the action plan for improvement during the next term. Next they shared their writing portfolio and the creative writing sample. I found that the students were excited and proud of their work, and their parents could see the growth their child had made, even during just one marking period.

Benefits of student-led conferencing

Since beginning student-led conferences, I have discovered their many benefits. They have helped me teach my students to take ownership of their learning and actions. I explain to them that the point of a parent-teacher conference is not to sit and tell secrets about them, but rather the meeting is about them—they need to be in it to hear what is said because in the real world, they will

be expected to meet and problem solve daily. Because students are often experiencing this inclusion for the first time, I find they frequently become excited and motivated by this new power and control.

As a teacher, I often explain to students that I don't "give" grades; rather, they earn them, but this is a hard concept for them to understand. With student-led conferences, I found that students took a great deal of ownership for their grades. By having to explain their grades during the conferences, students developed a more concrete picture of how their grade was determined, which prevented them from being "surprised" by it. Students also learned how to advocate for themselves at a younger age, and I found they were able to better articulate where they were struggling and to tell me how I could better support them. This was important because, as I always tell my students, I cannot help them if I don't know they need the help.

Involving students in the conference also helped them recognize and respect the collaborative efforts it takes to earn an education. Students saw firsthand the relationship between their families and their teacher and better appreciated the need for a strong working relationship between the two.

In the classroom, we are constantly challenged to create relevant and real-life teaching opportunities. What better way is there to teach real-life skills than through conferencing? Students analyze data, make inferences, and draw conclusions about their work. They use writing and organization skills to create their action plans and apply speaking and presentation skills as they participate in the actual conference.

Finally, one of my favorite benefits of student-led conferencing is that the number of surprise questions or requests during the conference is reduced. As a teacher, I always dreaded the questions parents would ask because many times what they were asking me were really questions their children could and should be answering. Student-led conferencing has helped me be better prepared for whatever might come up. I've also found

that less follow-up is needed when the student has participated in the actual conference. As questions or concerns come up, the student is there to lead the conversation, and I do not have to remember to talk to the student after the meeting. This helps me provide more individualized strategies based on each child's needs and in a timelier manner.

In my experience, parents are often blown away by the way their children are able to articulate their strengths and weaknesses. There is nothing more powerful than an eight-year-old explaining that in reading they can decode but have a harder time figuring what the text is about. By holding student-led conferences, parents are able to see a side of their child they might not previously have seen. For example, after one conference a mother said to me, "Wow, I knew that my son said reading was his worst subject, but I had no idea that he realized why. I love that he now has an action plan to help him improve."

Overall, student-led conferencing has helped me move from the traditional full day of meetings where I superficially and quickly told parents how their child was doing, to more collaborative, in-depth meetings where much more can be accomplished in a short amount of time. It has helped me build relationships with my students and their families by allowing me to interact on a more personal level with each of my students. Most importantly, student-led conferencing has helped me teach the skill of self-advocacy, because you are never too young to learn how to speak about and for yourself.

Student-Led Conferences in Action: Taking it to the High School

Pam Sessions, Media Specialist, Phoenix High School, Phoenix, OR

"I like the idea because I can share my own work and talk with my mother about it. I don't usually share so much about school when I get home; maybe a couple of things so this way we talk more about my work, goals, and grades together." PHS Junior

Today, the student-led conference process at Phoenix High School (OR) is a well-established part of the school's advisory program. When the state mandated that high schools implement and track a four-year plan for all students in 2007, student-led conferences were implemented as part of the advisory classes already in place. Even though the conferences were a natural fit with advisory, many staff members were skeptical, and one even boasted loudly, "You may get three parents that show up." From the first year on, student-led conferences at Phoenix High School have had an average attendance rate of 97%.

Conferences as part of advisory

Multi-grade advisory classes meet once a week for 45 minutes; students stay with the same advisor for the four years they attend PHS. Each year, students earn a quarter of a credit by completing a set of required activities that include a student-led conference; a full credit for advisory is required in order to graduate. Other yearly requirements include analyzing their transcript to help document progress toward graduation, reporting on state test scores and work sample assessments, updating a record of accomplishments (awards, activities, service, etc.), evaluating the career-related learning standards, and completing a summary reflection of the year. Advisors must sign off on a grade level checklist in order for students to receive the quarter credit each year.

A school counselor, Tami Ingwerson, serves as the director for the overall curriculum of the advisory class. She oversees the development of the lessons, activities, materials, etc., so that the advisors have only minimal prep work for the weekly class. She's also the one responsible for organizing and coordinating the process of the student-led conferences held each spring. Having watched this process develop over the years, she believes that "student-led conferences are a great opportunity to ensure that parents or guardians have the opportunity to sit down with their student to discuss the details of the school year that may not be talked about at home."

Goal setting

Leading up to the spring conference, students set and reflect upon both personal and academic goals each quarter. Students are asked to select a goal that can be completed by the end of the quarter and identify specific actions they will need to take in order to meet the goal. A progress check is done twice during the quarter that requires the students to list their efforts to date and what further work they can do prior to the end of the quarter. Goal reflections are completed at the end of each quarter, and students are asked:

- Did you meet your goal? Explain.

- What did you learn in the process of working toward meeting your goal?

- What obstacles did you encounter as you worked on your goal? Describe how you handled those obstacles.

Preparation for conferences

As the late April conference time draws near, advisors schedule conferences with their students. Postcards complete with mailing labels are given to each advisor to fill in and return to the main office, so they can be mailed home to parents. During this time, advisors also help students prepare for the conference. Because the majority of students attended TMS, they have experience leading a conference with their parents or guardians. Instead, preparation is focused on helping students collect and organize work, complete forms (one for each item in the agenda), reflect, and prepare to share the items from the "checklist" agenda related to their 4-year-plan requirements.

Results

How have staff responded to student-led conferences? After a recent round of conferences, Dea Baker, a long-time teacher at the school who freely admits that she was not completely sold on the idea, remarked, "Last night was amazing! My students were awesome. Most students spent 30-40 minutes with their parent(s) talking not only about where they are at right now, but where they would like to be in the future. I know that I was a skeptic in the beginning, but after last night, I can truly see the importance of the connection these kids are making with their parents. Listening to my kids talk to their parents with dignity and respect has completely changed my faith and belief in the ultimate goal of student-led conferences." Lonna Engle, a PHS instructional aide who also serves as an advisor, shared, "I love what I do as an advisor, and last night was a confirmation of this. The SLCs went great, the parents enjoyed themselves, and it was refreshing that they were not in a hurry to leave. I had kids and parents that stayed for over an hour. Not just one or two, but many!!! I felt like I should have gotten the coffee and cookies out. We had fun and I was also thrilled to sit and listen to the interaction that the kids had with their parents. Thanks for letting me be an advisor!"

Conclusion

So, is the time and effort devoted to the advisory program and SLCs worth it? Jani Hale, principal of Phoenix High School, believes it is. She states: "The greatest gift student-led conferences can give to our families is to provide a place to slow down, reflect, analyze the work to be done, and share dreams." She tells the story of a young man whose dream to be a professional studio musician was being sabotaged by his reluctance to keep up with day-to-day homework. By the end of the conference, the student and his father shared the same vision for his future and had worked through a plan to help the student succeed.

Isn't this much of what education should be about?

Figure 10-1 *Example of a high school SLC agenda*

Phoenix High School
Student-Led Conference Agenda

Welcome/Introduction

- Welcome everyone and introduce your parents/guardians to your advisor.
- Explain the reason for this conference: i.e.,: "…understand my current high school progress and how my progress fits with my future goals."

Review 4 Year Plan

- Discuss Academic and Personal Goals.
  - Did you meet your goals? Why or why not?
  - What helped you or what stood in your way?

- Discuss Transcript.
  - Explain credits needs for graduation and your progress.
    - Discuss specific requirements based on grade level and future goals.
  - Explain courses taken, grades earned, and credits received.
    - Use transcript to guide conversation.

- Discuss your current GPA.

- Discuss 3rd quarter report card.
  - Share how your progress aligns with your academic strengths and struggles and explain how this impacts your future goals.
  - Add the number of credits earned during the 3rd quarter to your transcript sheet.

- Review Essential Skills report (state assessments and required work samples).
  - Discuss Essential Skills report.
    - How have you scored on the tests in reading, writing, math, and science?
    - If you are not meeting benchmarks in some areas, what are you doing to improve your skills?

- Review your record of awards, accomplishments, experiences, and skills.
  - Talk about the activities in which you are or have been involved.
  - Share any recognition(s) that you have received.

- Share your best work sample.
  - Share your best piece of work from any subject and explain why you have included it in your 4-year-plan.

- Discuss your plans for after finishing high school.
  - Discuss career areas(s) of interest, post-secondary school options, and how you are preparing for life after high school.

- Complete the Quarter 3 section of the Career Related Learning Standards Evaluation.
  - Evaluate personal management, problem solving, communication and teamwork skills

- Share the Career Related Learning Experience Evaluation.
  - Describe the activity you participated in and what you learned.

- Discuss your grade-level-specific topic:
  - Seniors: Discuss Senior Project and Checklist Completions.
  - Juniors: Junior Career Paper and share ideas for Senior Project.
  - Sophomores: Discuss PSAT scores.
  - Freshman: Discuss Learning Styles Inventory from health class.

Registration for next year

- Share course requests for next year.
- Discuss how the courses/programs fit into your career path of interest and post-secondary plans.
- Discuss graduation requirements.

Concluding the Conference

- Ask parent or guardian if they have questions, comments, or suggestions.
- Thank everyone for attending.

Required

- Evaluation completed by parent
- Parent signature on 4-year-plan checklist

 Chapter 11

Student-Led Conferences 2.0

There is no question that the advance and increasing accessibility of technology is impacting student learning, and school organization and communication practices… and this impact will only continue to increase as schools work to prepare students for success in the 21st century.

Technology consultant Dedra Stafford (2012) states,

> As states move from widespread adoption of the Common Core State Standards (CCSS) to implementation, the realization is becoming clear that technology can no longer be a stand-alone opportunity used only in certain classrooms, but rather, it must become a blended part of all areas of thinking and learning. (para. 1)

> Our students will be expected to move beyond rote memorization and simple "plug and chug" problem solving. They will be asked to *think* and *understand* information, and technology will be an essential part of their CCSS journey. Students will be asked to produce and publish documents, interact and collaborate, communicate using Web tools, and evaluate information in multiple media formats. (para.2)

In addition to its impact on student learning, technology can also be used in a variety of ways to improve the student-led conferencing process. Chris Toy, a former middle school principal and a current certified Apple professional development consultant, explains:

SLCs are about home-school communication and as such, have been impacted by developments in communication technology. In many schools, both the process and materials of SLCs have been transformed by 21st century tools and resources. For example, multimedia digital files can replace paper portfolios that demonstrate student mastery with sights, sounds, and text. Moreover, these electronic portfolios can be shared anytime, anywhere, with anyone. The student's portfolio can be placed on a wiki or a blog, allowing others to leave feedback, comments, or to contribute additional resources.

Scheduling SLCs can be accomplished with one of several free online scheduling tools, such as doodle.com, which allows parents to go online to select an appointment time. Parents can also leave notes for the facilitator to confirm or ask questions. And, if a parent or other significant adult is unable to attend, online tools such as Skype, iChat, Adobe Connect, and Google chat make it possible to "be there" virtually. The integration of technology in SLCs is transforming home-school communication! (personal communication, June 11, 2012)

The two stories that follow illustrate how technology can be integrated into the student-led conferencing process. In the first one, a team of teachers from Maine share how their decision to implement digital portfolios has led to better communication with parents both during the year and SLCs. The second scenario tells the story of an Ohio middle school that moved from traditional parent-teacher conferences to student-led conferences to technology-enhanced SLCs. From these examples you will be able to glean ideas and strategies to use in creating a more technology-rich environment for the students in your school.

Student-Led Conferences in Action: Digital Portfolios

Amanda Blaine & Morgan Cuthbert
7th Grade Teachers at Harrison Middle
School, Yarmouth, Maine

Harrison Middle School has been holding SLCs for many years. In the past, our conferences went like this: The parents and student would arrive. The student would read from a prepared sheet that detailed successes in each subject, challenges, and goals for the future. The parents and teachers had an opportunity to weigh in. And this worked well for us in the past.

In 2002, the state of Maine initiated a one-to-one laptop program that today provides all 7th and 8th graders with Apple laptops, and most high schools have budgeted the funds needed to expand the program through 12th grade. Therefore, as we have become more and more involved with this laptop program, our students' work has shifted from paper products to digital products— Keynote presentations, YouTube videos, VoiceThread creations, etc.

Online portfolio system

At our final set of SLCs in 2011, many parents remarked that they did not see the amazing work their child had created with the computer. As a result, our charge was to create an online portfolio system for the 2011-2012 school year, and we set a goal that each student would have a fully functioning online portfolio to use in sharing classroom work and in reflecting on their progress during conferences with teachers and parents. Our desire was to have students update and share their work with their parents at least once a trimester, so that when it was time for SLCs, parents would already be familiar with their child's work. And while we hold the conferences twice a year (fall and spring), students would share their portfolio with their parents prior to grades coming out each trimester.

To begin, our team met in the summer of 2011 and brainstormed what information we wanted the portfolio to supply to us, the students, and the parents. We created a template for the portfolio (http://tinyurl.com/c5pr7bf) that included a section for each of the core subjects as well as the unified arts. The opening page is an "about me" section where students can add favorite quotes, photos, etc. After this year's experience in using the template, we plan to put a section for each trimester under each class instead of listing them by themes or units. We think this will make organization and viewing easier for the students and parents.

Google Day

To begin the process, we held a "Google Day" with each of the five teachers on our team hosting a different session in their room. As seventh graders in Maine, the students had just received their laptops, and this was a natural way to tap into their excitement about finally having their own computers. It also ensured that the students would have the basic skills needed to take advantage of our district's

Google platform. Homeroom groups rotated through the rooms with each teacher teaching a different aspect of computer use and Google. Over the course of the day, students not only learned computer basics but also how to navigate specific apps such as gmail, Google calendar, and Google Docs.

One of the sessions was on the portfolio site. Although students didn't have any work to upload yet, they used this session to download the template, personalize the "about you" section, rename the site according to our convention (last name, portfolio, graduation year), and share the site with teachers and parents. The sites are secure and only visible to sanctioned viewers. A hopeful outgrowth of this work is that the administration is currently looking at the possibility of using this portfolio system beginning in 5th grade and following the students as they progress through the grades.

Modeling use of the system and reflecting on work

As the first trimester progressed, we modeled and taught the students how to use the system and how to reflect upon their work. We set aside about 40 minutes the first time they had a completed project to upload. During this first session, they learned how to scan work, rename the file, and put it on the site in the appropriate place. We've learned that giving dedicated class time every so often is necessary to keep the portfolio up-to-date and more effective than asking students to wait to comment on projects completed in the past. We've also allowed students to take the lead in demonstrating how to use the tools. If a student is familiar with a tool or process, we ask him or her to demonstrate and teach all of us. In this way, we've been able to learn as we go along, rather than needing to be the experts on everything before sharing with our students. The students teaching us gain experience in communicating to a group and a boost in self-esteem as they share their expertise.

Conclusion

As we near the end of our first year of this process, parent feedback is consistent with this sentiment: "I like being able to see the work in one place. A huge bonus is that a large binder will not come home at the end of the year, one that we will feel conflicted about going through and then tossing much of. Also, seeing the scoring rubrics is helpful."

We've noticed that having the online portfolio pushes us as teachers to create products that are lasting and authentic. We're motivated to help students take advantage of Web 2.0 tools that they can use to share their online portfolios with their parents and teachers.

"We're Making it Work"

Student-Led Conferences in Action: With a Technological Twist

Jay Clark, Principal,
Van Buren Middle School
Van Buren, OH

We patiently wait outside the door of our son's team conference room. At 8:45 p.m., with military precision, the door swings open, out comes another set of eighth grade parents, and Mr. Smith glances our way welcoming us into the science classroom. We sit down across the table from the teachers. Mrs. Jackson starts the timer sitting at the edge of the black tabletop and begins telling us about our son's progress in language arts. She quickly discusses his vocabulary test scores and how she's enjoyed reading his writing. She turns her head to Ms. Kern, who tells us that she's concerned with test scores in U.S. History, but that our son's homework completion and quiz scores will give him a strong 'A'

average. Mr. Smith takes over telling us a brief story about our son's work on a mineral lab. His comments blend into Mr. Mitchell wrapping up the whirlwind conference saying that our son has a deep understanding of equations, and he's certain that the advanced high school math courses would be a good placement.

Whew. Did anyone take a breath? Mr. Smith stood up as did we, and as we walked out the door, we turned to thank the teachers, who were taking drinks from their travel mugs and resetting the timer for the next round of machine-gun feedback.

This scenario at Van Buren Middle School, a small rural school in northwest Ohio, was our best attempt to facilitate parent-teacher conferences. Then, at our state middle level association conference in 2006, some staff members attended a presentation by an urban school that shared their success with student-led conferences. We embraced the concept that fall for two reasons: First, all parents and guardians would have the opportunity to attend a conference. Because we had a limited number of team conference slots, we maintained a "waiting list" and even had to turn some parents away from having a conference; plus those that were scheduled resembled the assembly line described above. Second, making students the focus of the conference would greatly change the purpose and scope of the conference. SLCs would give students stronger ownership of their learning, provide them with a structure to discuss school with their parents, and give them an authentic audience for their practice of skills such as presenting and writing.

After determining the logistics and scheduling, we began the SLC process with students writing letters of invitation that were mailed home. Today, the letter is still an important part of the process, although it has morphed to meet different language arts standards, such as using propaganda techniques to convince their parents to attend. For a week or so prior to conference days, teams prepare students by creating talking points or scripts and discuss how the students will welcome their parents. While many details have evolved over the years, the big

idea remains and continues to drive the success of this format—the purpose is to provide an opportunity for students and parents to discuss education and, more importantly, set goals together. We now have more than enough time slots to allow all parents to attend. Conferences last varying amounts of time—anywhere from fifteen minutes to more than an hour. In fact, because this format is so flexible and efficient, we have even blocked off a few hours on one of the days to schedule professional development meetings.

Initially, we held the conferences in our school cafeteria. Each team had a part of the large room, and there was a central table lined with boxes of student portfolio folders. When a family entered, the student would pick up his or her portfolio, sit down, and the conference would begin. Teachers watched the different conferences and approached the family once the student had been given ample time to present his work. The teachers then discussed the child's progress in their class with both the student and parents and then moved on to another family.

Problems with using the cafeteria included the numerous distractions and the noise level as there could be more than 20 conferences occurring simultaneously. Later, we moved the conferences to each team's science lab—larger classrooms with tables accommodating parents in more comfortable and intimate settings. Because we shared only a few teachers between teams, this worked well.

Evaluations of the conference format were collected over the first two years. Our first year, 54% of parents cited interacting with their child as the top positive aspect of the move from traditional conferences, and 17% cited the lack of teacher input throughout the conference to be the biggest drawback of the change. A parent of a high-achieving student stopped me soon after the conference days. She shared that, thinking it would be a waste of her time because she talked with her son daily about school, she had not understood the need for a conference. However, after the conference, she had new insights about her son's learning, and they both had a deeper conversation as a result of the structure.

Since we began student-led conferences, technology has contributed greatly to our evolution. Before our one-to-one computing program was implemented, we used our online grade book during the conferences by setting up desktop computers along the side of the conference area. Students had work samples—projects, writing, tests and quizzes—in a file folder to use as visual aids as they talked with their parents.

Part of our school's shared vision is that technology is embedded in all that we do. Our use of technology throughout the school day is exceptional to visitors, but it is routine to our staff and students. Five years after starting student-led conferences, we began our one-to-one computing initiative with all middle school students loaned netbook computers to use throughout the school year. Our content management system (CMS) is central to the one-to-one computing idea. We had been using Moodle as our CMS for a number of years, so all of the teachers had a basic understanding of its functions, and it now serves as our students' dashboard while at school. Each class has a page, and students use a digital portfolio to collect their work—this is replacing the file folder portfolios used during SLCs.

Student-led conferences also give us a terrific opportunity to educate parents on how technology has changed our students' school day. The conference provides a structured environment for a student to give mom and dad a glimpse into how school has evolved since their time as students. During the conference, students use their netbooks to show their parents notes from a specific day on the class Moodle page, to demonstrate a variety of digital media used in the class and/or to watch a video product completed as part of a collaborative group project. For a parent to see how an assignment may be completed electronically, submitted through the CMS, and then see the letter grade and comments on the electronic grade book is powerful.

The initial shock of moving from traditional to student-led conferences was difficult for some parents, although our students embraced it very quickly. Staff members were happy to see this change as the student-led format is much more personal and thorough. Having to face a team of four or five teachers from across a table often put parents on the defensive from the beginning, and those team conferences could be very contentious. Understandably, the timer (yes, we used timers) and the rushed tempo caused parents to perceive the conferences as cold and impersonal.

A student-led conference literally brings the most important person to the table—the student.

 Chapter 12

FAQs about Student-Led Conferences

1. Can low-achieving or special-needs students conduct effective conferences?

Absolutely. The vast majority of low-achieving and/or special needs students do well with the SLC format. In fact, preparing for a SLC can often motivate lower-achieving students. The student responsibility and ownership required in the conference setting often causes those students with historical poor achievement because of behavioral reasons to complete assignments and put more effort into their work. For many such students, this is the first time they have had a voice to discuss their own learning.

If the student is on an IEP, the self-reflections allow him to highlight his strengths and set achievable goals. Depending on the disability, the student may work with both a content area teacher and the special education teacher to select appropriate portfolio samples. We have had students on IEPs successfully participate in SLCs, often to the joy of their parents. Depending on the child's abilities and skills, the conference facilitator, special education teacher, or an aide may choose to remain throughout the entire conference to help the student discuss work and share work samples.

2. What happens if parents don't attend?

Schools do need to have a plan to deal with this possibility because SLCs are, first of all, learning experiences that *all* students should experience. If a parent does not show up, the first step is to call the parent to reschedule if at all possible. Infrequently, but on occasion, a parent will not respond to this request. If this happens, we find a time that a "substitute" parent can listen to the student present his or her portfolio. One option is to use a staff member, who can be anyone from an administrator to a favorite teacher to the secretary to an instructional aide—preferably someone who already has a relationship with the student. Another viable option is for regularly scheduled substitute teachers (ones well known by the school) to serve as conference "listeners." Oftentimes, depending on the class, they may find themselves with time available during the teachers' scheduled prep periods. It works best to hold these catch-up conferences within the week or so following the regularly scheduled times. Also, depending on the situation and student involved, you may want to consider sending the portfolio home with the student, so he or she can conference with the parent in the home setting.

3. How does an ELL conference work?

Our school has a significant percentage of English Language Learners, and SLCs dramatically increased conference attendance of non-English speaking parents. Because communication with their child is in their primary language, they are much less intimidated in the school setting than if they had to converse in English with teachers. Because the student is well-prepared, the facilitator need not be bilingual; the student serves as a translator if necessary. Tone of voice and body language convey the essence of the conference amazingly well to the facilitator.

If the student had very limited ability to speak English, we did our best to pair him or her with a facilitator or an aide who spoke the native language. This helped not only with the preparation for the conference, but also in better preparing the student to share the portfolio. Goals written in the native language also helped the parents to better understand and support the students in achieving goals.

4. How is a student with high absenteeism successful?

There are many reasons for a student to be chronically absent. If the student has a chronic illness, he or she may be receiving tutoring to stay current with classroom assignments, and conference preparation can become part of that service. If the absenteeism is due more to apathy or a problematic home situation, student work generally reflects this. Usually, issues at home will come up during the conference (whether with the parent or another adult) as the student explains why there is little or no evidence of growth. Asking students to look at their performance, explain the consequences of their absenteeism, decide what needs to be done about it, and then collaboratively coming up with a plan to address the issue can help students see how to overcome obstacles in their lives.

5. How do we bring a reluctant teacher on board?

Change is hard for everyone, and it is important for school leaders to listen to the staff's concerns. We started small, with a few teachers willing to pilot the SLC model. Their success proved contagious, and the next year more teachers volunteered to try it. By the third year, when the site-council decided everyone would participate, all teachers had the necessary training and materials. Teachers who were still reluctant were asked to give it their best effort and were promised that the process would be evaluated after the conferences were over. We found by listening to concerns and making adjustments that did not conflict with the basic philosophy behind the conferences, school-wide support for the conferences grew; within a few years the process was simply part of the school's standard operating procedures.

6. How much preparation time does it take to get ready?

It is possible to do much of the conference preparation as part of regular classroom time. For instance, it takes about 15-20 minutes after a major project to complete a self-reflection. Prior to the conferences, classroom teachers will also need to designate time for students to select work samples, complete summary reflections, fill out a cover sheet, and practice sharing their pieces from that class.

Finding the time to meet with the conference facilitator depends on the organizational structure chosen by the school. We found that gathering work, organizing the portfolio, writing the goals, and practicing presentations took about 30 minutes a day during the five to seven days before the conference. Since TMS had a scheduled homeroom period, students met during that time to complete those tasks. Schools that do not have similar time built into their schedules may wish to run a special schedule during conference preparation time; reducing each class by five minutes or so to create a preparation period seems to work well. Remember that although preparing for SLCs takes more time than for traditional parent-teacher conferences, the benefits are far greater.

7. Are there ways we can reduce the demands on teachers' time when preparing for conferences?

Early preparation and no surprises are the keys. The process will be easier if someone in the building serves as an overseer for the logistics to ensure necessary materials are ready when needed, siblings are scheduled on the same day, and staff is well aware of deadlines through a timeline published early in the year. At TMS, the principal was responsible for this, with some responsibilities delegated as appropriate. In other schools, an instructional coach, a media specialist, or a counselor serves in this capacity.

8. **How do we respond to a parent's request to replace a student-led conference with an individual parent-teacher conference?**

   Parents who want a conference with a teacher should be given one, but it should not take the place of the SLC. While one purpose of the conference is communication between home and school, SLCs have another purpose, too—providing students with an opportunity to develop and use reflection, communication, and presentation skills in an authentic setting. Explaining this greater purpose to parents often helps them understand the value of the process.

   However, for parents who insist on speaking with a teacher, we first remind them of the drop-in time before and after the SLC. For most parents, this fills their needs. If a one-on-one private setting is necessary, then teachers schedule a meeting with the parent at a mutually convenient time.

9. **How do we handle parents who are aggressive or negative during the conference?**

   In our experience, parents rarely act negatively toward the child during the conference. At the infrequent times when this has occurred, the facilitator joined the conference, redirected the discussion, and allowed the student to take control of the conference once again. That is generally effective. The well-being of the student is the responsibility of the facilitator, so if a parent persists in berating a student, the facilitator may need to halt the conference to prevent emotional damage. If the parent seems to be having issues with a particular teacher, a one-on-one meeting with that teacher to resolve issues may be appropriate. The student can then complete the conference in a safe environment at a later time. Some schools have dealt with this issue by making sure that an administrator, dean, or counselor is always free during scheduled conferences and can be called upon for immediate help if necessary.

10. I want to try this but don't think we're ready for a school-wide approach. How can I enlist the support of my principal to give it a try?

If at all possible, find a like-minded colleague to work with. The SLC process is much easier to implement if you have someone with whom to share its challenges and joys. Develop a plan and discuss with your principal why you want to do this, what you want to accomplish, and how this will help your students make better progress in their learning. You or your team can offer to pilot a program for your school, present a plan of how it would work, and explain how you would evaluate its success. Be specific about what support and resources you would need to implement the plan—and be prepared to put in the extra hours required to make it succeed. Generally, after seeing it in action, administrators (and other teachers) see the value and are willing to support the process.

11. How do you inform parents about the change to student-led conferences?

Today, SLCs are so prevalent at TMS that parents rarely question the process. However, as with any new innovation a school embarks upon, clear communication with parents is a necessity. In the beginning, we communicated the new procedures with parents through as many means as possible: the school website, the newsletter, letters sent home from individual teachers, PTA meetings, etc. Two to three weeks prior to the conference, parents were notified of conference times through post cards mailed home. If you are the first school in your district to initiate SLCs, we recommend you send several written notices home in addition to holding an informational evening for interested parents. The more parents understand the intent and process of SLCs, the more supportive they will be.

12. How should the room be arranged for conferences?

If you will have multiple conferences taking place at the same time, room arrangement is important. We found the most effective organization is having one station set up in each corner of the room. Each station consists of a small table with four or five chairs. Place the chairs with their backs to the center of the room to give a sense of privacy for each of the conference groups.

13. Who facilitates the conference?

The role of the facilitator during the conference is to provide support, ensure the conference gets off to a good start, and step in to help the student only if the situation becomes difficult. After the initial introductions, especially at the middle and high school levels, the facilitator should move out of the way and allow the student to run the conference. If possible, the facilitator should rejoin the conference to assist during the goal-setting process.

14. Why does the facilitator step away for most of the conference?

It's important to remember that the purpose of SLCs is not only for the student to share information with parents in a neutral setting, but also to give students an opportunity to practice their skills of communication and organization as they talk about their learning and articulate what's important to them. This means that the students need to be in charge of the conferences.

If the facilitator remains at the table, the student may be inhibited and/ or the parents may turn to the adult to ask questions, leaving the student out of the process. Experience taught us that for middle grades and high school students, the majority do quite well on their own. Generally, for younger elementary students, more adult support is needed. Knowing their students best, classroom teachers should determine the extent of their role in the conference.

15. How do I deal with a problem student in a conference format?

Amazingly, students rise to the occasion of SLCs. Likely, all of us share the experience of a student who "goofed off" during practice and then surprised us when he came through in the end. But that doesn't make it any easier to handle a student who is uncooperative during practice time. If that situation occurs, we recommend you approach it as you would a difficult student in your classroom: talk with the student in private, give reminders and redirections, or contact parents if appropriate. If you have a difficult student and you would like to confer with the parents in addition to the SLC, use the cover sheet comment section to ask the parents to visit you during a drop-in time.

16. How often do students meet with the facilitator to prepare?

This varies depending on the format you use for the conference. At TMS, we met for 35-minute periods with our conference advisor groups about seven or eight times prior to the conference.

17. Why do all of your certified staff act as facilitators?

This decision grew out of a desire for equity. By involving every certified staff member in the process, we shared the workload and reduced the size of each group. Another plus was that this gave all certified staff a clear understanding of the process and a feeling of involvement. The downside was that there were times, especially in the evening schedule, when no appropriate person was available to help with a problem. We found it helpful to invite a district office administrator to be on site at this time. There is no one right way; other schools have organized their conferences by teams, by a particular period (i.e., everyone facilitates their 2nd period class), advisories, or some other structure that works for their situation.

18. How did you find time to develop this process?

Finding time for development is critical for the process to be successful. Fortunately for us, our district had a one-hour delayed start dedicated to professional development on Monday mornings, which we used for SLC planning. Prior to implementing this process, review your inservice calendar to see where time is available. In several districts we have worked with, the school principal obtained the superintendent's permission for an early release afternoon to plan the process. Because time is essential, be sure that whatever time you do have is productive. Be organized with specific goals for each meeting. Having a draft of a plan to use as a starting point goes a long way toward ensuring that time is used effectively.

19. When is the best time to hold SLCs?

The time of the conference depends on the purpose for the conference. Ideally, it's nice to do one during both the fall and spring. Fall conferences focus on growth to occur during the remainder of the school year and have the advantage of:

- Providing students with a focus and direction early in the year

- Allowing students an opportunity to demonstrate their efforts at the beginning of the year

- Supplying parents with important information about both their child and the school

- Giving plenty of time for implementing goals

Spring conferences serve more as a summary and a celebration and are helpful because they:

- Show a student's growth over time

- Emphasize important accomplishments made during the year

- Give a clear picture of the child's academic progress

- Allow for goals to be set for the next school year

One is not necessarily better than the other; they are simply done for different reasons. In making the decision about when to hold conferences, determine your purpose before setting your dates.

20. How can students use the SLC process to share their progress toward meeting state standards?

At TMS, each spring our eighth graders used a more formal version of SLCs to review their academic growth during middle school, their progress toward meeting state standards, and their goals for high school and beyond. Parents or guardians, other family members, and friends were welcomed to these presentations. Facilitating the conference was whoever had facilitated their student-led conferences, and at least one other certified or classified staff member also attended.

Because students had kept selected work samples from sixth and seventh grade in their portfolios, they were able to illustrate and discuss their growth in learning during the middle grades. Students also shared results from state-required work samples and assessment tests. This information was then used as a springboard for the students to discuss their goals for high school and their most current post-secondary plans. We also encouraged the students to choose a project, product, or performance completed during their middle school years to "showcase" and share why it had special meaning to them.

References

Baber, S., & Tolensky, L. (1996). Student led conferences. Retrieved from: http://www.
yrbe.edu.on.ca/~cecn/slc/home.htm

Benson, B., & Barnett, S. (1998). *Student-led conferencing using show-case portfolios.*
Thousand Oaks, CA: Corwin Press.

Berckemeyer, J., & Kinney, P. (2005). *The what, why, & how of student-led conferences.*
Westerville, OH: National Middle School Association.

Chappuis, J., Stiggins, R. J., Chappuis, S., & Arter, J. (2012). *Classroom assessment
FOR student learning: Doing it right—Using it well* (2nd ed.). Upper Saddle River,
NJ: Pearson Education

Costa, A. L. (1989). Re-assessing assessment. *Educational Leadership, 46*(2), 1.

Countryman, L. L., & Schroder, M. (1996). When students lead parent-teacher
conferences. *Educational Leadership, 53*(7), 64–68.

Cromwell, S. (2010). Student-led conferences: A growing trend. *Education World.*
Retrieved from http://www.educationworld.com/a_admin/admin/admin112.
shtml#top

Culver, L., & Cousino, G. (2000, January). Building a partnership: Student-led
conferences engage students in evaluation of progress. *Schools in the Middle, 9*(5),
13–15.

Czikszentmikaly, M. (1990). *Flow: The psychology of optimal experience.* New York:
Harper Perennial.

Hoeppner, J. T. (2009). *Student-led conferences and their purposes, structure, and
content: A multiple case study approach.* WI: (Eric Document Reproduction Service
No. ED513222.)

Kinney, P., Munroe, M. B., & Sessions, P. (2000). A school-wide approach to student-led conferences: A practitioner's guide. Westerville, OH: National Middle School Association.

National Association of Secondary School Principals. (2011). *Breaking Ranks: The comprehensive framework for school improvement*. Reston, VA: Author.

National Association of Secondary School Principals. (2009). *Breaking Ranks: A field guide for leading change*. Reston, VA: Author.

National Middle School Association. (2010). *This we believe: Keys to educating young adolescents*. Westerville, OH: Author.

Paulson, F. L, & Paulson, P. R. (1994). *Student-led portfolio conferences*. (Report No. TM022503). OR: (Eric Document Reproduction Service No. ED 377241).

Smith, M., & Ylvisaker, M. (Eds.). (1993). *Teachers' voices: Portfolios in the classroom*. Berkeley, CA: National Writing Project.

Stafford, D. (May 2012). Blending technology into the Common Core Standards. *Middle Level Leader*. Retrieved from http://www.nassp.org/tabid/3788/default. aspx?topic=Blending_Technology_into_the_Common_Core_Standards.

Stiggins, R. J. (1994). *Student-centered classroom assessment*. New Jersey: Prentice-Hall.

Stiggins, R. J. (1999). Assessment, student confidence, and school success. *Phi Delta Kappan, 81*(3), 191.

Additional Resources

Print Resources

Association for Curriculum and Supervision Development. (2005). *Where students lead, achievement follows.* Conference report retrieved from http://www.ascd.org/publications/newsletters/education-update/jan05/vol47/num01/Where-Students-Lead,-Achievement-Follows.aspx

Countryman, L. L., & Schroeder, M. (1996). When students lead parent-teacher conferences. *Educational Leadership, 53*(7), 64–68.

Dickinson, K. (2004). Student-led conferences at the secondary level. Retrieved fromhttp://education.jhu.edu/newhorizons/strategies/topics/Assessment%20Alternatives/dickinson.htm

Elliott, L. (2012). *Accidental techie to the rescue!* Peterborough, NH: Crystal Springs Books.

Garrison, C., Chandler, D., & Ehringhaus. (2009). *Effective classroom assessment: Linking assessment with instruction.* Westerville, OH: National Middle School Association.

Goodman, Amy. (2008). Student-led, teacher-supported conferences: Improving communication across an urban district. *Middle School Journal, 39*(3), 48–54.

Kinney, P. (2005). Letting students take the lead. *Principal Leadership, 6*(2), 33–36.

Schurr, S. (2012). *Authentic assessment: Active, engaging product and performance measures.* Westerville, OH: Association for Middle Level Education.

Shulkind, S. B. (2008). New conversations, student-led conferences. *Principal Leadership, 9*(1), 54–58.

Tuttle, H.G. (2007). Digital age assessment in technology and learning. Retrieved from http://www.techlearning.com/article/digital-age-assessment/44127

Digital Portfolio Resources

Creating portfolios in several software applications: (http://electronicportfolios.com)

Electronic Portfolios in the K-12 classroom: www.educationworld.com/a_tech/tech/tech111.shtml

Forms and Handouts

These forms may serve as starting points for creating your own forms and handouts for the student-led conference process at your school. Included are a variety of self-reflections, cover sheets, and informational memos to the staff concerning the myriad details of running successful SLCs. Additional forms and handouts are available at www.amle.org/SLC_Kinney.

Table of Contents

Conference Forms

Subject Area Cover Sheets

Staff Memos Communicating SLC Process

Self-Reflection Examples

Student Procedures for Conferencing

1. Introduce your parents or guardian to your facilitator.

2. Explain you will be sharing your fall portfolio during the conference.

3. Briefly review the Table of Contents to give an overview of what is in your portfolio.

4. Read your "Dear Parent" letter.

5. Present your work.
   - Share the information on the cover sheet
   - For each piece share:
     - What the assignment was
     - What knowledge or skills you learned by doing it
     - What process you went through to complete the piece
     - Key portions of your self-reflection by reading them aloud

6. Share your report card with your parents.

7. Goal Setting
   - Explain the two goals you have set.
   - Write a third goal with your parents.

8. Parent homework letter
   - Give your parents their "assignment sheet" and ask them whether they would be willing to write you a note as explained on the sheet. What they write can be kept at home or returned to school to put in your portfolio.

9. Closing
   - Thank your parents for attending your conference.

Portfolio Table of Contents
Student-Led Conferences
Talent Middle School

Name: _____ Grade: _____

Date: _____

Dear Parent Letter

- Core (Reading, Writing, Social Studies) Cover Sheet
    - ○ Work sample #1: _____
    - ○ Work sample #2: _____
    - ○ Work sample #3: _____
    - ○ Work sample #4: _____

- Mathematics Cover Sheet
    - ○ Work sample #1: _____
    - ○ Work sample #2: _____

- Science or Health Cover Sheet
    - ○ Work sample #1: _____
    - ○ Work sample #2: _____

- Elective Cover Sheet
    - ○ Work sample #1: _____
    - ○ Work sample #2: _____

- PE or Second Elective Cover Sheet
    - ○ Work sample #1: _____
    - ○ Work sample #2: _____

- Report Card

- Goals for Success

- Parent Homework Letter

Missing Work!

Name: _____   Teacher: _____

Assignment Title: _____   Subject: _____

Assignment Due Date: _____

I was given the opportunity to do this work but either did not complete
it or turn it in because:

_____

_____

_____

_____

_____

_____

_____

_____

_____

_____

Goals for Success

Name: _____ Date: _____

My strengths are:

    A.

    B.

    C.

I need to work on:

    A.

    B.

    C.

First Goal: _____

_____

To achieve this goal, I will

    A.

    B.

Second Goal: _____

_____

To achieve this goal, I will

    A.

    B.

Third Goal: _____

_____

To achieve this goal, I will

    A.

    B.

People who can help me attain these goals are:

Distractions that may get in the way of accomplishing these goals are:

_____	_____	_____
Student Signature	Parent Signature	Facilitator

Goals for Success: Revisited

Name: _____ Date: _____

First Goal: _____

_____

List two things you have done (or are doing) to meet this goal.

    A.

    B.

What are two things you can do (or continue to do) in the next few weeks
to make sure you are successful in meeting this goal?

    A.

    B.

Circle the word that describes your effort to date in meeting Goal 1:

None   Little   Some   Good   Excellent

Second Goal: _____

_____

List two things you have done (or are doing) to meet this goal.

    A.

    B.

What are two things you can do (or continue to do) in the next few weeks
to make sure you are successful in meeting this goal

    A.

    B.

Circle the word that describes your effort to date in meeting Goal 2:

None   Little   Some   Good   Excellent

Third Goal: _____

_____

List two things you have done (or are doing) to meet this goal.

    A.

    B.

What are two things you can do (or continue to do) in the next few weeks
to make sure you are successful in meeting this goal?

    A.

    B.

Circle the word that describes your effort to date in meeting Goal 3:

None   Little   Some   Good   Excellent

Core

(Reading, Writing, Speaking, and Social Studies) Cover Sheet

Name: _____ Date: _____

Teacher: _____ Grade: _____

Class Expectations:

+ exceeds expectations   √ meets expectations   − needs improvement

Self Teacher

_____ _____   Completes classwork/homework on time

_____ _____   Works independently

_____ _____   Works well in a group

_____ _____   Manages behavior appropriately

_____ _____   Comes to class prepared to learn

Comments: _____

_____

_____

_____

_____

Math Class

Cover Sheet

Name: _____ Date: _____

Course: _____ Grade: _____

Class Expectations:

+ exceeds expectations   √ meets expectations   – needs improvement

Student Teacher

_____ _____ Responsibility for assigned tasks

_____ _____ Classroom behavior

Comments: _____

_____

_____

_____

_____

_____

_____

_____

_____

Science Class

Cover Sheet

Name: _____   Date: _____

Teacher: _____   Grade: _____

Class Expectations:

+ exceeds expectations   √ meets expectations   – needs improvement

Student Teacher

_____ _____ Works well with lab partners

_____ _____ Works safely with lab equipment

_____ _____ Stays on task and completes work

Comments: _____

_____

_____

_____

_____

_____

_____

Health Class

Cover Sheet

Name: _____ Date: _____

Teacher: _____ Grade: _____

Class Expectations:

+ exceeds expectations   √ meets expectations   − needs improvement

Student Teacher

_____ _____ Works well independently

_____ _____ Works well with others

_____ _____ Completes assignments on time

_____ _____ Uses time wisely in class

_____ _____ Has a positive attitude

_____ _____ Treats people with respect

Missing assignments: _____

Comments: _____

_____

_____

_____

127

Elective Classes

Cover Sheet

Name: _____   Date: _____

Teacher: _____   Grade: _____

Electives:

❏ Art/Crafts   ❏ Band   ❏ Choir

❏ Computers   ❏ Journalism   ❏ Applied Math/Sci (Tech)

❏ Aide   ❏ Spanish   ❏ Intro to Languages

Class Expectations:

+ exceeds expectations   √ meets expectations   − needs improvement

Student Teacher

_____ _____   Shows respect for others, self, and property

_____ _____   Stays on task to complete work

Comments: _____

_____

_____

_____

_____

Contents of Student-Led Conference Portfolio

Table of Contents: *(lists all items in portfolio)*

Dear Parent Letter: *(serves as an icebreaker, introduces parents to conference, written in core classes)*

Work Samples:
- Core Cover Sheet *(completed in core class by both teacher and student)*
    - 2 to 4 samples of core class work with self-reflections
- Science or Health Cover Sheet *(completed in class by both teacher and student)*
    - 1 or 2 samples of science or health class work with self-reflections
- Math Cover Sheet *(completed by both teacher and student)*
    - 1 or 2 samples of math class work with self-reflections
- PE Cover Sheet *(completed by both teacher and student)*
    - 1 or 2 samples of PE class work with self-reflections
- Elective Cover Sheet *(completed by both teacher and student)*
    - 1or 2 samples of elective class work with self-reflections

Missing Work:
Any uncompleted work should be indicated by a "Missing Work" form to be filled out by the student in the class the work was assigned.

Goals for Success: *(to be completed with conference facilitator)*
All students should have two goals and plans for their accomplishment written on their goal sheet. In conjunction with their parents, students will write third goal during the conference. Students should have a third goal and plan ready to use in case parents do not have one to suggest. For easy "access," the goal could be written on the inside of the portfolio folder.

Report Card:
This will be given to facilitators on the Friday before conferences begin.

Parent Homework Letter: *(given to facilitators and then to students for placing in their folders).* Parents are encouraged (but not required) in a self-explanatory letter to respond to their child's conference in writing.

Scheduling Student-Led Conferences

Date for scheduling: _____

You will be scheduling your conferences on Wednesday during your facilitator meetings with students. For those new to the process, the easiest way to schedule is to call one student at a time to the back of the room while having the rest of the class work quietly on something. While not necessary, some have found it helpful to write the student's appointment time and day on a piece of paper, so the student can give his or her parents advance notice. Schedules and postcards will be in your mailboxes on Wednesday morning. Before scheduling your conferences, please review the following information:

- Official times for conferences are:
  - ❏ Monday 7:30 a.m. – 6:30 p.m. *(breaks: 11:00 a.m. – 12:30 p.m., 3:00 p.m. – 4:30 p.m.)*
  - ❏ Tuesday 10:00 a.m. – 8:00 p.m. *(breaks: 12:00 p.m. – 1:30 p.m., 3:00 p.m. – 5:00 p.m.)*
  - ❏ Wednesday 8:30 a.m. – 1:30 a.m.

- As a general rule, you may schedule up to three conferences at a time, four during the evening slots. Please do not schedule more than that unless it just cannot be avoided.

- You must be in your room during drop-in times.

- Families will be scheduled through the office on Monday and Tuesday. Therefore, when you get your schedules for Wednesday, you may have conferences already scheduled for students with siblings. Do not change a scheduled student without checking with student services first.

- You are responsible for filling out a postcard for each of your students (even those scheduled through the office). This includes putting the mailing label on the back. Blue cards are printed in Spanish.

- Schedule all of your students, even those that are absent. Parents will be able to call the office to change their appointment if necessary.

- At the end of your facilitator time on Wednesday, return your postcards and schedules to Student Services.

- Schedules will be kept in student services until just prior to the conferences, so the office can make changes if a parent should call.

Countdown to Conferences!

By Wednesday, each facilitator will receive a packet containing the following:

- Folders to use for portfolios
- Student Procedure Sheets
- Table of Content Sheets
- Goals for Success Sheets
- Parent Homework Letter
- Reminder invitations for the conference

1. **Classroom Practice:** Students should come to their facilitators on Monday the 15th having practiced sharing their work samples with their classroom teachers. For each sample, the student should be able to share:

   - What the assignment was
   - The knowledge or skills learned by doing the work
   - The process used to complete the sample
   - A key portion of the self-reflection *(highlighting works well)*

2. **Student Procedures for Conferencing**: Use the Student Procedure Sheet *(see page 119)* to help your students learn the process to follow during the SLC. Please be sure your students are familiar with the steps. Stapling the sheet to the inside cover of the portfolio may prove helpful to students.

3. **Goal Setting:** If your students have trouble thinking of their strengths and areas for growth, they can get ideas by reading through their self-reflections. Ask students to be specific in setting their goals. "Math" is not a goal, but "Turning in my math homework on time" is.

4. **Parent Homework Letter:** Ask your students to read the form. Emphasize that it is perfectly fine if their parents choose not to write a letter, and ensure there will be no repercussions. They should simply ask their parents to "do their homework." The letters from the parents can be kept at home or returned to school to be put in the portfolio.

5. **Facilitator Role during Conferences:** As a facilitator, you are responsible for being present during the conferences but not necessarily a "part" of the conference. At the beginning, students should introduce you to their parent/guardian. Because you may have up to four conferences happening simultaneously, monitor them by carefully listening and be ready to help out if you see a student struggling. Near the conference's end, touch base with the parents. If at all possible, try to join each conference during

the goal-setting process and be sure the proper items are taken and left. Although it is fine to step outside your room for a few minutes to get something, for the most part, you should be visible. Please do not use the time for lengthy conversations with other teachers.

6. **What Stays and What Goes:** All student work should be left in the portfolio because some of it may be used as an official work sample as required by the state. Parents may take home:

   - The report card
   - A copy of the Goal Sheet
   - Parent Homework Letter assignment

There will be some other information for parents to take home *(i.e., parent newsletter, etc.)*. You will get copies of it by Monday morning.

7. **Drop-in Time:** You must be in your room and available during all drop-in times.

8. **Practicing:**
   - Monday: Organize the portfolio and fill out the table of contents.
   - Tuesday: Focus on the goal-setting process
   - Wednesday: The entire school will view a short video that models a SLC; finish goal setting
   - Thursday and Friday: Practice, practice, practice. Break students into groups of two or three to role play the conference. Changing groups daily helps eliminate the "boredom" factor. Every student should have the opportunity to practice his or her entire conference two or three times.

9. **Reminder Invitations:** Have your students fill these out on Friday the 19th and take home as a reminder to parents.

10. **Celebration:** You will meet with your facilitator group on Wednesday, Dec. 1 for a celebration; goodies will be provided.

11. **"Unloading" the work:** Thursday, Dec. 2, the work samples will be returned to teachers. Students will report to 1st period for attendance. After the morning announcements, teachers will dismiss students to go to their facilitator to pick up their portfolios, and then students will immediately return to class. As they go to classes during the day, they will return work to their teachers. Students may take home any work left over at the end of the day. PE and electives teachers: let students know to bring you their work if you need it returned.

Wrap-Up of
Student Led Conferences

A big THANK YOU to everyone for helping our conference process go smoothly. Our parent feedback forms show that 63% of parents strongly agreed and 34% agreed that student-led conferences were valuable and informative!

Please attend to the following details so we can wrap up our conferences for this year.

- If you have a folder for a student who did not show up for the conference and you do not have a conference scheduled for that student, give the folder to Student Services, who will attempt to reschedule the conference. If that is not possible, we will need a teacher, another certified staff member, a support staff person, or a substitute to listen to the student's conference. Every student will have an opportunity to share. Please let the office know when you are available to help.

- Please complete the staff feedback form and turn it in by Thursday.

- On Wednesday, December 1, we will run a facilitator schedule. Orally debrief your students about how the conferences went. We will provide ice cream bars as a treat for a job well done.

- Facilitators: please remove the yellow "Goals for Success" copy from the portfolios and place them in the student's conference file. We will have a Revisiting Goals Day in about 6 weeks.

- Thursday, December 2, will be used as "Unloading" Day. Students will pick up their portfolios from their facilitators in the morning and return work samples to teachers through the day. Any work not needed in the future should be sent home with the student.

Summary Self-Reflection: Writing

Name: _____ Date: _____

1. List the pieces of writing you completed this trimester:

   Topic/Title   Mode

   1.

   2.

   3.

2. What piece of writing do you consider your most effective?

3. Why? What did you do as a writer to make it effective?
   Cite examples.

4. What new skills do you need to work on as a writer?
   Who can help you with this skill?

5. What are your writing goals for the rest of the year?
   How will you accomplish them?

Summary Self-Reflection: Math

Complete the following letter and staple it to your best, worst, and most challenging papers from math class this trimester. Make sure to label your papers "best", "worst", and "most challenging." This is YOUR letter, so you may change or add topics or issues as needed.

Dear _____ ,

In math class, the topics we've studied are...

I learned that...

I chose_____ as my best
work for the following three reasons:

      1.

      2.

      3.

I chose_____ as my worst
work for the following three reasons:

      1.

      2.

      3.

I chose_____ as my most
challenging work for the following three reasons:

      1.

      2.

      3.

I believe I have progressed in the area of...

I still I need to work on...

Sincerely,

Self-Reflection on an Individual Piece of Writing

Name: _____ Date: _____

Title of Piece: _____ Mode of Piece: _____

Look at carefully at your writing. Answer the following questions thoughtfully.

1. What do you see as the special strengths of this paper?

2. What was especially important when you were writing this piece?

3. What have you learned about writing from your work on this piece?

4. What skills does this piece of writing show you possess?

5. What skills does this piece of writing show you need to develop further?

6. If you could go on with this piece, what would you do?

7. Additional comments you would like me to know about you and your writing:

Summary Self-Reflection: Reading

Read over your reading responses, the list of books you have read, and your reading work. As you answer these questions, think about how you have grown as a reader this trimester.

What has been the most helpful to you in the way we do reading workshop in our classroom? How has it helped you as a reader?

What are your strengths as a reader?

What would you like to improve as a reader?

What's the best book you've read this trimester? What makes this the best one for you?

What's the most significant thing you learned from this book and/or discovered about yourself as you read it?

What genres of books would you like to read in the future? What can I (the teacher) help you do as a reader?

What goals do you plan for yourself as a reader?

Self-Reflection on a Project: Social Studies

Name: _____ Date: _____

Class: Social Studies   Type of Project: Research Paper

Title of Project: Ancient Egypt: 3100 B.C. – 30 B.C.

(Students: This is a model to guide you in sharing with your parents during the conference. Feel free to think of your own catchy beginning!)

As you read through my exploration of _____,
sit back, relax, and take a trip back into the times of pharaohs, pyramids, and ancient mysteries. I chose the topic of _____
because _____.

I started my research on *(month, day, year)* and completed it on *(month, day, year)*. The only information I knew about before I began my in-depth study was _____
_____.

I began my research by _____. I found it easy
to _____ but I got frustrated when _____
_____.

Some interesting information I learned was _____
_____.
One thing I learned that surprised me was _____
_____.

The project I made was _____.
It enhanced my study of _____
by _____.

If I did this research and project again, I would _____
_____.

(End with a conclusion that is catchy and fun and makes the reader want to read your thoughts and information about your topic.)

Self-Reflection on a Science Lab

Name: _____ Date: _____

Class: Science   Type of Project: 3 Science Experiments

Title of Project: 3 Rocketry Experiments

Describe the 3 lab experiments we have completed during our Rocketry Unit.
What have you learned?

List some of the variables that may have altered the final outcomes of the
launch angle and volume tests.

Have you enjoyed this study so far? Why or why not?

Several scientific principles were explored in the Diving Tube Lab. List them.
How does this lab apply to life outside the science classroom?

I struggled with…

I really enjoyed…

Self-Reflection on a Project: Health

Name: _____   Date: _____

Class: Health   Type of Project: Decision Tree

Title of Project: An Important Decision

My situation was: _____

_____.

The choices I had were: _____

_____.

The choice I made was: _____

_____.

I chose it because: _____

_____.

The easiest part of this assignment was _____ *because:*

_____.

The hardest part was _____ *because:*

_____.

If I did this project again, I would: _____

_____.

Self-Reflection: Physical Education

Name: _____ Date: _____

1. My strengths in Physical Education are:

2. I can improve in Physical Education by...
   (behavior, participation, effort, honesty, sportsmanship, etc.)

3. I can improve my personal fitness level during Physical Education class by:

4. I can further enhance my personal fitness outside of PE class by:

Student Self-Reflection/Teacher Evaluation: Physical Education

Name: _____ Date: _____

Teacher: _____

Level of cooperation with other students:	Effort: I participate to the best of my ability:
Student: 1 2 3 4 5 6 Teacher: 1 2 3 4 5 6	Student: 1 2 3 4 5 6 Teacher: 1 2 3 4 5 6
Turned in make-up for absences: Student: 1 2 3 4 5 6 Teacher: 1 2 3 4 5 6	Dressed daily in proper uniform: Student: 1 2 3 4 5 6 Teacher: 1 2 3 4 5 6
Level of honesty and fair play: Student: 1 2 3 4 5 6 Teacher: 1 2 3 4 5 6	On time to class: Student: 1 2 3 4 5 6 Teacher: 1 2 3 4 5 6
Listening Skills: I follow directions. Student: 1 2 3 4 5 6 Teacher: 1 2 3 4 5 6	Golden Rule: I treat others the way I would like to be treated. Student: 1 2 3 4 5 6

Scoring Guide

6/Exemplary: Work at this level is both exceptional and memorable. It shows a distinctive and sophisticated application of knowledge and skills.

5/Strong: Work at this level exceeds the standard. It shows a thorough and effective application of knowledge and skills.

4/Proficient: Work at this level meets the standard. It is acceptable work that demonstrates application of essential knowledge and skills. Minor errors or omissions do not detract from the overall quality.

3/Developing: Getting there! Work at this level does not meet the standard. It shows basic but inconsistent application of knowledge and skills. Work has minor errors or omissions that detract from the overall quality. It needs further development.

2/Emerging: Work at this level shows partial application of knowledge and skills. It is typically superficial, fragmented or incomplete, and needs considerable development before reflecting the proficient level. Work at this level may contain errors and omissions.

1/Beginning: The work shows little or no application of knowledge and skills. Work at this level contains major errors or omissions.

Self-Reflection for an Oral Presentation

Name: _____   Date: _____

Class: _____   Topic: _____

Directions: Take a few minutes to reflect on your presentation and then answer the following questions

1. Thinking back over your presentation, what were your thoughts and reactions about how you did?

2. What do you think were the strengths of your presentation? *(Refer to the scoring guide to be specific)*

3. If you could redo your presentation, what would you like to do differently?

4. What visual aid(s) and/or enhancers did you use in this speech? How were they effective? *(Size, clarity, ease of use, referring to them during the presentation, etc.)*

5. What are some goals *(or areas to improve)* you'd like to see yourself accomplish for your next speech?

CPSIA information can be obtained at www.ICGtesting.com
Printed in the USA
BVOW021222021212

307024BV00004B/8/P

9 781560 902492